How Did You Do That!

Stories of Going for It

Presented by Gail Kingsbury

Yinspire Media
info@yinspiremedia.com
www.YinspireMedia.com

_____

Producer: Ruby Yeh

Editorial Director: AJ Harper

Print Management: The Book Lab

Cover Design: Pearl Planet Designs

Book Design & Typesetting: Chinook Design, Inc.

ISBN-13: 978-0981970882

Printed in the United States of America

Contents

Contents

Introduction

Gail Kingsbury

When people accomplish something they once thought impossible, their lives become an inspirational touchstone for those of us who want to achieve something amazing, too. We hold up their happy ending as a shining example of what is possible in our own lives—but what about the rest of their story? What about the moments leading up to the success? How did they get from "before" to "after?"

Brainstorming titles for our book about extraordinary accomplishments—*this book*—we came up with all sorts of crazy ideas, but nothing really clicked until we realized that it all boiled down to the question we were asking the authors: "How did you do that?" We were so excited to find our title in that question, because it's *the* question people ask when someone does something remarkable, something truly awe-inspiring.

How did you heal your heart, solve that problem or defy the odds? How did you find the courage to jump off that cliff, face your fears and really go for your dream?

For the past twenty years I have produced events for the personal and professional development industry, creating opportunities for amazing people to share their message and change the lives of hundreds of thousands of others. Over the years, I've come to understand that while letting go of the "how" can be a powerful tool in your own story of manifestation, learning *how others* achieved success busts the myth that you are somehow different from them, that you are *less than*—less capable, less worthy, less talented, less everything you need to be to make your own vision a reality. When all you know is the beginning and ending of a success story, getting your own "happy ending" can seem like a fairy tale. But when you know how *they* did it, the story becomes real—and so does your dream.

> *When all you know is the beginning and ending of a success story, getting your own "happy ending" can seem like a fairy tale. But when you know how they did it, the story becomes real—and so does your dream.*

How Did You Do That! is a collection of stories about people who achieved lifelong goals, found lost loves, built fortunes, experienced medical miracles, discovered their true callings and made a difference. They are stories of humble beginnings and heroic endings, but they are also stories of "how"—how they did it, and how you can do it, too.

Together, the co-authors in this book make up a chorus of possibility. They are a diverse group not only in terms of age, race, geographic location and focus, but also in their approach, their "how." Some pushed forward on nothing but fumes and faith; others gathered a supportive posse of mentors, colleagues and friends. Some stayed the course; others changed tactics along the way. Some chose a conventional route; others blazed a trail from start to finish.

The common thread in all of these stories is that all of our amazing contributors found a way to make their dreams come true. And, in reading their stories, you will find *your* way.

Foreword

Mark Victor Hansen

S tories are the greatest tools for changing lives. From the beginning of time, good stories have motivated people to not only see what is possible, but also to take action so that possibility becomes reality. A good story can have a massive impact on society. The transformational power of story blows my mind.

Julius Caesar wrote enthralling stories of his conquests in Gaul that made him popular enough to be named Dictator of Rome. *Uncle Tom's Cabin* fired up the Abolitionists' cause and influenced President Abraham Lincoln to write the Emancipation Proclamation. Mahatma Gandhi's writings inspired Dr. Martin Luther King, Jr. and Nelson Mandela to overcome injustice and change the world through nonviolence.

Since we released the first *Chicken Soup for the Soul* seventeen years ago, Jack Canfield and I have had the privilege of hearing thousands of stories about ordinary people doing extraordinary things. We've also had the honor of meeting thousands of people who have been so moved by a *Chicken Soup for the Soul* story, they made radical changes in their own lives—and, in some cases, radically changed the lives of thousands more.

At one of our recent seminars, Jack and I were seated on either side of a lovely woman with an amazing story of personal triumph. Just over seven years ago, she was pregnant and totally alone, with no husband and no parents, and had to give up her baby for adoption. Later, with no job or resources, she ate out of the garbage behind McDonald's and bathed in their bathroom. Then one day she saw a library, and thought perhaps she could go in and hide, maybe take a nap.

One inspiring story can change a life. Many inspiring stories can change the whole world.

"I saw a table marked, 'Inspiration Books' and I picked up your book. The first story I read was 'Puppies for Sale' by Dan Clark, and that story inspired me to change my life," she said. "Today, I'm happily married with three kids, and I started Chicken Soup for the Soul Kitchens, which feed ten thousand people every month in Ohio."

One inspiring story can change a life. Many inspiring stories can change the whole world. One of my favorite examples of the impact of narrative story happened not too long ago, when Jack and I were signing books like crazy at BookExpo America. With eight hundred people waiting, Jack pulled me aside and said, "You're not going to believe this story." He introduced me to Bob Deggas, who promptly said, "You saved my country."

When we launched our first book, Jack and I set the goal of changing the world one story at a time. It's one thing to set that goal, and something else entirely to deliver on the promise. Yet there was Bob, telling us how *Chicken Soup for the Soul* stories saved his whole country. "I'm from Lebanon, and I work at Lebanon University," he began. "When we were fighting Syria, I would have ten thousand kids come to the University every night, and I would read one story out loud every night. They were living under threat of death. They knew they could be imprisoned, tortured, maimed at any time, but your stories gave them the courage to defend our country."

Ten thousand meals served to impoverished families every month. Ten thousand students bolstered to defend their country. This is the tremendous power of a good story. If one good story can make this significant impact, imagine what an entire book full of them could do for you.

How Did You Do That! is *that* book—that book you've been looking for that could inspire you to change your own life, the book you'll keep forever, returning to its dog-eared pages for ideas and inspiration. In this collection of amazing true stories, you'll find the courage to finally go for it and *do that* thing you've been yearning to do, joining the dozens of men and women in this book who made the leap, found their path, kept the faith, knocked down walls, climbed the mountain and broke through to a new life. Are you ready to be truly inspired?

A Seeker's Pilgrimage

Barbara De Angelis, PhD

From the time I was very young, as far back as I can remember, I have always been searching for answers. Not superficial answers, but deep answers to the most significant questions like, *"What are we doing here? What am I doing here? What is my purpose? How can I make sense of all the suffering around me?"*

For me a lot of this questioning began when I was a very young child because my parents were in a very, very unhappy marriage. I watched the sadness around me and something about it just didn't make any sense to me. And as I grew a little older, I had a strong conviction that how I saw most people living—getting up, going to work, accumulating material possessions, trying to fit in to society and its expectations—was not all that life was supposed to be about.

When I entered my very early teens, I became very depressed, indrawn and confused. I couldn't understand why the harsh world I saw around me didn't look anything like the vision I had deep within of what was possible. By the time I was in my senior year of high school, I was at a tremendous spiritual crossroads, a place of true crisis. I had achieved everything academically and socially that I could have up to that point in my life, and yet felt empty. I thought perhaps if I left the East Coast, things would be different. I had been offered early acceptance to the University of Wisconsin in Madison. Without really understanding why, I accepted the offer.

This feeling of isolation, of confusion, this sense that there were answers and mysteries I had to comprehend created a tremendous fire in me—the fire of longing that all seekers have: to find a path, to find a teacher, to go on a search for answers whether or not you know where that search is going to lead.

Sometimes we are drawn to our destiny by guidance whose voice is not loud, but very subtle. The voice of the divine is a whisper, not a shout. Often, we are waiting for guidance as if

---

Sometimes we are drawn to our destiny by guidance whose voice is not loud, but very subtle.

---

we are supposed to hear a loud announcement. That's not how things happen. The voice of the Great Consciousness is very, very tender and almost silent. It's not something you hear, bur rather something you feel in the heart.

A few weeks after arriving at the University on the way to one of my classes, I noticed a poster on a bulletin board. The poster contained a picture of an Indian saint and the words, "Learn to meditate." I can hardly talk about this now without choking up, because this poster was the lamp I had been looking for to guide me home. It was the poster of Maharishi Mahesh Yogi, the founder of Transcendental Meditation, who had come to the West to teach people how to meditate and find inner happiness. Up until that moment, I'd had no connection or exposure to anything Indian, but the moment I saw the radiant face of this great sage, I felt like my entire world turned upside down. I knew I had to go to this lecture.

I remember exactly where I sat in the hall that night. I remember one of Maharishi's students who gave the lecture, and I remember everything he said. I was eighteen years old, and yet every word he said was like nectar. It all made complete sense:

the idea that within me was a place that was the source of energy, intelligence, happiness, creativity, wisdom, love; that the blocks that didn't allow me to access that place were what caused my suffering; and that this was an ancient understanding, and that learning to go within and find a way to tap into that systemically would change my life. I knew it was true and it was as if for the first time, I was hearing someone speak a language that I understood.

I instantly signed up to be instructed in meditation. The student price was thirty-five dollars—in those days a fortune for me. So I took every penny I had, and I didn't eat for a week to save up the money. Two weeks later I remember walking two miles to the place where they were performing meditation instruction. And again, I will never forget the experience of going into a

---

It was like opening a door that had been locked my whole life, a door that upon opening, instantly revealed what felt like lifetimes of remembrance, and from that moment my life was never the same.

---

room with the man who had been trained as one of Maharishi's meditation teachers, sitting down and closing my eyes and being shown a way to go within. It was like opening a door that had been locked my whole life, a door that upon opening, instantly revealed what felt like lifetimes of remembrance, and from that moment my life was never the same.

My whole life shifted—how I approached everything, how I thought about everything, how I felt about myself, how I felt about my family, how I felt about the future. It was as if life had been in black and white and suddenly became in color! It was a profound, instant and unbelievable awakening for me.

When I found out that Maharishi Mahesh Yogi himself was coming to Humboldt State College in Northern California for a month that summer I knew that I had to make the pilgrimage. I drove with friends in a Volkswagen van from Philadelphia all the way to Northern California where again, I had a totally life changing experience and recognized my first true spiritual teacher.

That is just the very beginning of a piece of the story of my finding the doorway to the inner world. From that point on everything in my life accelerated at a tremendous rate. I decided I would become a teacher of meditation. What followed from that were many, many years of spending up to a year at a time studying with Maharishi in Europe, being trained as a meditation teacher, then becoming an advanced teacher and practitioner. I immersed myself in very deep and serious spiritual practice.

At the time if you asked me, would I be doing anything other than that, I would have said of course not. Would I ever write a book? It wasn't even on my mind. Would I ever be on television? It would have seemed absurd. I had no personal goals for myself at all; I wanted people to find inner peace. I wanted people to find a connection to the inner source of joy and wisdom. It made complete sense to me that the world's suffering was because people were disconnected from that source, had forgotten it even existed. That's all I believed in and cared about, and what I focused on for many years.

The amazing thing about the way our lives work is that just as when a bud is really ready to open, and the flower emerges, you couldn't have imagined something so beautiful was inside. Just as anything that begins as a seed, and is invisible in the earth can grow in to an entire tree, so I see that during those early years on my spiritual path, I was being cultivated and prepared for something beyond my comprehension, beyond anything I could have imagined at the time.

By the time I was in my late twenties I found myself feeling a longing to go back to school and get a master's degree in communication and psychology. I didn't understand why—I just felt that I should do it. I also began looking at how, although my spiritual development was quite advanced, I hadn't integrated my spiritual understanding and expansion of consciousness into my relationships, and my emotional life.

So this determination to integrate spirituality into the rest of my life became a new path I knew I needed to follow. I began to take experiential psychology workshops and watched what was being taught. Somehow I knew there was a different and better way to take people on a transformational journey. Somehow I knew how to take people much deeper than I saw the other

---

Suddenly my career was born—not from any desire to be famous, but from a desire to help people find peace.

---

workshop leaders taking them, how to create an environment of so much love and safety that people could experience profound emotional shifts in a short period of time. It was as if this tremendous knowledge began to pour through me, which Maharishi had predicted during the many years I spent at his side.

When you go to the source of everything, Maharishi had explained, knowledge will begin to emerge from within you. You will have access to the storehouse of all wisdom. I felt that beginning to happen to me. I just began to know things, understand things; Writing began to pour from me onto the page. I was flooded with knowingness. At first I really didn't know what to do with it. But then something compelled me to hold my first workshop. Something said, "You need to teach—not meditation, but something different that is based on all that has been revealed to you through your spiritual development." So I invited eighteen people into my living room in Los Angeles for my first class, a workshop about relationships and spirituality. Those eighteen people loved it and told several people each, and the next time I offered the workshop there were forty people who wanted to sign up, and soon I had to rent a hall for my seminars.

Suddenly my career was born—not from any desire to be famous, but from a desire to help people find peace. My destiny began to unfold in front of me. I could feel that the more I offered what I knew, the more doors opened up for me. Before I knew it I had an extremely successful seminar business, and bestselling books. I began my radio and television career, and became well known and watched by millions of people.

And yet, nothing really changed from that very first moment when I saw the poster and followed the calling in my heart. Nothing changed from the first moments in my youth when I would sit alone in my room longing to know the answers to life's greatest mysteries. That fire to seek truth, to dig deep, to contact the unlimited world within—that fire was always blazing and was the source of everything that I accomplished, everything I offered, everything that has impacted millions of people around the world. The way I became a spiritual transformational teacher was by undergoing my own profound spiritual transformation.

All of us arrive at times in our lives that are challenging, that don't make sense, times when we may feel confused, or even lost. Many people just freeze in those moments. It is as if we are waiting for someone to give us a map, an itinerary, a sort of cosmic GPS that will tell us how to proceed. This is not going to happen. The process of being willing to take those leaps and follow those silent whispers that lead us forward is the very process of interacting with the divine, and that is what we, as seekers, are being asked to do. When you discover the patience and vision to walk courageously on your own path of awakening, even if you cannot see more than one step in front of you, you *will* be transformed as you go, and you will end up exactly where you need to be.

Barbara De Angelis

Barbara De Angelis, PhD, is one of the most influential teachers of our time in the field of personal and spiritual growth. For the past thirty years, she has reached tens of millions of people throughout the world with her positive messages about love, happiness and the search for meaning in our lives. As a best-selling author, popular television personality and sought after motivational speaker, Barbara is legendary in the field of personal transformation as one of the first people to popularize the idea of self-help in the 1980's, and as one of the first nationally recognized female motivational teachers on television.

Barbara is the author of fourteen best-selling books which have sold over ten million copies and been published throughout the world in twenty languages. She has had an amazing four #1 New York Times Bestsellers. Her most recent book is HOW DID I GET HERE? Finding Your Way To Renewed Hope and Happiness When Life and Love Take Unexpected Turns, *which has won numerous awards.*

Barbara's television career has been just as successful as her publishing career. She hosted her own TV shows on CBS and CNN, her own special on PBS and wrote and produced the award-winning TV infomercial, "Making Love Work," which was seen by over fifty million people throughout the world. Barbara has appeared regularly on TV shows including Oprah, The Today Show, Good Morning America, *and* The View.

Barbara is renowned as a charismatic and moving speaker, and is the recipient of the highest honor from Toastmasters International as their Golden Gavel Award Winner for 2007—one of only five women to receive this award in Toastmaster's fifty year history for being one of the most outstanding speakers of the century. Barbara is currently president of Shakti Communications Incorporated, dedicated to bringing enlightened messages to the world through all electronic and print mediums, as well as through Barbara's unique coaching and seminar program "Transformation From the Inside Out." Barbara lives in Santa Barbara, California. To learn more about Barbara visit www. BarbaraDeAngelis.com

Anything and Everything IS Possible

Mark Victor Hansen

Most people know about my accomplishments as co-creator of the *Chicken Soup for the Soul* series, but they don't know how I got my start as a public speaker. They probably also do not know how broke I was, how inexperienced I was, or how determined I was to succeed when I realized what I *really* wanted to do with my life, and set out on the path that led me to this moment. I'd like to share this story with you, because I want to prove to you that no matter what your circumstances are now, anything and everything you want is completely possible. Take a moment to take in that truth. Because when I say anything and everything, I do mean anything and everything—including that big dream, that secret dream, that "impossible" dream you've been carrying around in your heart.

Thirty-five years ago, my company went bankrupt. We made geodesic domes, spherical buildings made out of triangles invented by my teacher, Buckminster Fuller. We built all kinds of cool stuff in New York—the Wall Street Racquet Club, the aviaries at the New York Botanical Gardens. I was twenty-six years old with an exciting business, and I was really rocking it. But I ended up rocking us right *out of* business, to the tune of two million dollars. I was so busted I had to check a book out of the library about how to go bankrupt. I moved to Hicksville, New York, on

Long Island, the poorest place I had ever lived, and rented an apartment with four other guys. I was determined to succeed, to pay back the money I'd blown screwing up the company and also to build a new, profitable career. But first I needed a job.

Despite the fact that I had double master's degrees, the only job I could get was unloading toilet paper off a railroad car for two dollars and fourteen cents an hour. I still remember the first

---

Because when I say anything and everything, I do mean anything and everything—including that big dream, that secret dream, that "impossible" dream you've been carrying around in your heart.

---

day I arrived at the job site wearing a suit, dress shoes and my white London Fog trench coat. I didn't wear the clothes because I wanted to impress anybody or pretend I was somewhere else; I wore them because I had nothing else to wear.

"You don't look dressed right for this job," the supervisor said.

"I won't be here long," I replied. "I just have to eat."

During this time, I realized that what I *really* wanted was to become a public speaker. But all the speakers I knew or heard of were older lawyers, doctors or celebrities, and I didn't fit any of those categories. So once I got clear about what I wanted to do, I sat down with my four roommates over breakfast and asked them if they knew any young public speakers. One of them said, "There's this guy out in Suffolk County, Chip Collins. He's in real estate and he's a speaker." So I sought him out. I watched Chip work for three hours, wowing the audience. I knew right away I wanted him to mentor me. As everyone filtered out, I walked up to Chip, thanked him for the talk and said, "Look, I'm broke. Would you take me to lunch and teach me how to do this business?" Amazingly enough, Chip said yes. I could see why he was so successful; he was interesting, fun and charismatic. Over lunch he gave me the hard facts, explaining that my chances of making it as a speaker were about one in a thousand. But he could see I was determined to make it, so he told me what to do.

"Go after the insurance market. It's a bottomless pit for motivational speaking," he said. "They never run out of need because they turn over ninety percent of their sales force every year."

Insurance? I didn't know anything about insurance. I asked Chip how I could get people to hire me to give a speech when I didn't know anyone in that industry, and, more importantly, how could I give a motivational speech about selling insurance when I didn't even know what a premium was?

"Don't worry about it, you'll learn," he said. "You'll learn because you have to. Just keep knocking on doors." He told me I should get four people to sign up for one talk, and give them an under-market rate of twenty-five dollars a slot. He also explained how to approach prospects, and that I could get the money in advance by asking, "Would you like to cut the check or should I

"Don't worry about it, you'll learn," he said. "You'll learn because you have to. Just keep knocking on doors."

---

have your secretary cut it?" Chip said I should contact him when I had sold four talks. "By the way," he added, "I'm gone for two weeks at Disneyland with my kids, and I don't expect to see you when I get back."

The next day I went out and knocked on ten doors. Nine people turned me down, but the tenth guy said yes. His name was Tony, and he was a director at Metropolitan. He got a kick out of my "should I have your secretary cut the check" approach and signed up for a talk. He also gave me a directory of contacts and said, "Just tell 'em Tony sent you." I drove to one office building after another in my permanently air-conditioned Volkswagen with no windshield wipers, a car that looked so junky I had to park it far from the offices where I cold-called and gave my talks. I knocked on doors until I got one person to say yes, and then another, and then another.

By the time Chip got back, I had sold twenty-eight talks. I could tell he was surprised to see me, but he simply said, "Now it's time to raise your rate." We decided we would meet at a diner

---

Obstacles are just opportunities to come up with clever solutions and genius ideas.

---

every Friday afternoon and he'd teach me how to really make it as a public speaker. The first week he gave me a sales goal, but when I slid into the booth that Friday I had to tell him I had come up short.

"You can't go home until you reach your goal," he said.

"But it's Friday afternoon. Everyone's gone home," I replied.

Then Chip gave me a first lesson in how to bust through perceived barriers and limitations. He said, "Right now, in New York, there is someone you can sell a talk to—tonight. Get in your car and drive to an office building with only one car in the parking lot. That car belongs to the boss, and since everyone else has gone home for the weekend, you won't have to get past the gatekeepers or bodyguards. You can go straight to the boss."

When faced with obstacles, those who are passionate and determined to succeed will innovate; they will find a way to get it done. Obstacles are just opportunities to come up with clever solutions and genius ideas. Because Chip refused to let me go home until I had made my quota, I was forced to try a different approach, and from that experience I learned that there is always a way and I started to get a glimpse of the truth—that anything and everything *is* possible. That night I went out and made my goal. After that experience, I went out on the following Friday night from six to ten o'clock and hit all my sales for that week in four hours. From that point on, I trained with Chip; I learned the business and I knocked on door after door after door.

Even though I was broke, even though I was an amateur in a competitive field, I had rockets of desire. When your desire is high enough, there are no limits. You become a fully functioning, self-actualizing person. It's the Law of Attraction at work—the universe resonates with your desire and says, "yes." Within two months of that first lunch with Chip, I had enough money to put a deposit down on a leased car. Within a year, I owned a home in Garden City. That year two colleagues each put up a credit

> *When your desire is high enough, there are no limits. You become a fully functioning, self-actualizing person.*

card so that I could attend the National Speaker's Association conference, where I learned about multi-author books. We sold twenty thousand copies of our first book, *Stand Up and Speak*, from the platform in one year. I thought, "Life couldn't get any better than this." But it did.

Thirty-five years after launching my speaking career, I've talked to five million people all over the world and sold over one hundred and fifty-seven million books. Thirty-five years after I started out earning twenty-five dollars an hour, I now earn between twenty and fifty thousand an hour. Thirty-five years after he bought me lunch, Chip is my best friend and I still talk to him almost every single day—and I've since bought Chip a lot of lunches!

There's one right, perfect, easy and acceptable way for everyone to become a millionaire. Speaking and entrepreneurship are perfect for me because my passion is helping people live a masterful, exciting, purposeful life. I want that outcome for you, too. I want you to have everything you desire, anything you can imagine, and all that you need to help you lead a joyful life.

Whatever your circumstances, nothing is out of your reach. Whatever you don't know, you'll learn. As Chip said, you'll learn because you have to. Anything and everything IS possible for you. Just keep knocking on doors!

Mark Victor Hansen is America's "Ambassador of Possibility." For more than thirty years, Mark has focused solely on helping organizations, and people from all walks of life, to reshape their personal vision of what is possible. His powerful messages of possibility, opportunity and action have helped create startling and powerful change in thousands of organizations and millions of individuals worldwide. A passionate philanthropist and humanitarian, he works tirelessly for organizations such as Habitat for Humanity, The American Red Cross, Childhelp USA and others. In the year 2000, Mark was rewarded with the prestigious Horatio Alger Award.

Co-creator of the landmark Chicken Soup for the Soul *series, Mark is a best-selling author, sought-after keynote speaker and marketing maven. Mark's books include* The Power of Focus, The Aladdin Factor, Dare to Win *and* The One Minute Millionaire: The Enlightened Way to Wealth, *co-authored with Robert G. Allen. Mark is the founder of MEGA Book Marketing University and Building Your MEGA Speaking Empire, annual conferences where Mark coaches and teaches new and aspiring authors, speakers and experts on building lucrative publishing and speaking careers.*

Mark serves as Chief Executive Officer of M.V. Hansen & Associates, Inc., co-founder of Chicken Soup for the Soul Enterprises, Inc. and President of One Minute Millionaire, LLC. He has been featured on numerous television programs, including Oprah, CNN *and* The Today Show, *and in countless print publications, including* TIME Magazine, US News & World Report, USA Today, The New York Times *and* Entrepreneur. *To learn more about Mark and his programs, visit www. MarkVictorHansen.com.*

Cocooning My Way to Oprah

Maritza Parra

My fate was sealed. A native of Texas, I had the same aspirations as many of my friends: grow up, get married and have children. Like most Hispanic women, I had been told over and over that my purpose in life was to fulfill these maternal expectations, and I spent most of my adult life trying to do just that. It wasn't that I didn't have other goals, too. I did, and I accomplished many of them. But marrying and having children was the ultimate goal. The problem was it wasn't *my* ultimate goal, although I didn't know that for a long time.

As I searched for the "man of my dreams," in the back of my mind—and at the core of my heart—I knew something was missing. It was a nagging feeling, a hole that needed to be filled. I did my best to fill it with boyfriends, things and accomplishments, assuming it would be filled and stop nagging the moment I said, "I do."

When I got married, I thought, "Finally. I'm fulfilling my duties as a woman." Thinking of my marriage as a duty—even if only for a moment—should have tipped me off that I was not following my true path. But I continued to ignore the little inner voice that kept trying to tell me there was more to life, more to *me*. It never even occurred to me that my only duty was to my own self-development, that the singular goal of becoming a wife and mother would not bring me the happiness I had been yearning for.

For the next six years, my husband and I tried everything we could to have kids. Fertility issues eventually led us down the path of in vitro fertilization (IVF), at which point my doctor advised me to quit my job in an effort to remove undue stress. I followed instructions, dedicated myself to getting pregnant and tried to stay positive. Nothing worked. No matter what I did, no matter how hard I tried to keep the faith, I just could not get

---

It never even occurred to me that my only duty was to my own self-development, that the singular goal of becoming a wife and mother would not bring me the happiness I had been yearning for.

---

pregnant. I felt as though I was letting everyone down, especially my husband. My whole life had been dedicated to the goal of creating a family, and I couldn't get the "job" done. And then one day my husband came home and asked me for a divorce.

It came out of nowhere and blindsided me, and before I could wrap my head around it, I was sitting before a judge watching my hopes and dreams disappear with the stroke of a pen. In five minutes, my marriage was over. I drove home from the courthouse in a daze, wondering how I would keep the house without a job. I had given up everything for the dream, and the dream had died. What was I supposed to do next?

When I got home I went straight for the backyard, looking for calm. I listened to the water we kept for the wild deer that often found their way onto our property. As it bubbled and flowed, I felt the familiar black hole in my chest, the sense that something was missing. There was no escaping it now. "No one is coming to save you," I thought. All this time I had been looking for someone to save me, to fill in the hole. I was alone. No one was coming. I fell to the ground, crawled into a little ball and started to cry.

In that moment I realized I had to save myself. I could not articulate how I would save myself, but for the first time in my life, I was listening to that little voice inside me. Operating on pure instinct, I cocooned.

First, I got a job to pay the bills. Then, I shut out the world that had fed my misguided focus and insecurities. I turned off the TV and limited my interaction with other media. Instead, I listened to inspirational stories on tape and on the radio. I took up journaling, started practicing meditation and began studying spirituality and healing. I studied with mentors, leading experts in the field of self-empowerment. I traveled, pursued what I enjoyed, I played. I befriended myself again.

One year later I was happier than I had ever been. It dawned on me that a lot of women would benefit from cocooning. I knew that when you teach, you master what you've learned. So I decided to hold a free meeting to share the principles of

---

In that moment I realized I had to save myself.

---

self-empowerment that had helped me find my true purpose. I reserved a community room near my house, posted the meeting announcement online, and, on the day of the first meeting, put up a poster with a picture of a girl meditating, so people could find the room.

Four people came to my first meeting. I talked about meditation, the Law of Attraction, being in the now and positive thinking. When the meeting was over, I said, "See you next week," not knowing if anyone would show up. The next week six people came, and the week after that, ten. Every week more people would show up than the week before, until we had to move from the community room to a nearby art gallery. I got better at leading the meetings. I started making more elaborate presentations, complete with handouts. I was having so much fun. I was really, truly happy for the first time in my life. I had emerged from the cocoon as a joyful woman living an authentic life aligned with my passion. Amazing things happened after I started giving back through my free weekly meetings. One story is so amazing, people ask me to tell it over and over. When the group grew to over two hundred people, I noticed not everyone could attend the meeting every week. Some of the participants had friends and loved ones who wanted to come but lived too far away. Then it hit me: what if I created a virtual podcast so that everyone could benefit from the meetings?

And then one day, while home at a time when I was normally out, the phone rang. I noticed the caller ID: Harpo, Inc., Oprah Winfrey's production company. I thought, "Yeah, that could happen."

"Hi Maritza, my name is Corny Koehl. I'm a producer with "The Soul Series," an XM Radio show on *Oprah & Friends*. Do you have a few minutes?" she asked. "We heard about your weekly meetings in San Antonio, and we want to hear more about your story." Corny asked me to share the stories from my group, how

---

It was one of those moments when you look down on yourself and see how far you've come. It was only two short years ago that I was crying like a baby on my back lawn.

---

they used the Law of Attraction, their successes, their healing and their transformations. Later, when Corny said, "Oprah would like to interview you on her radio show," I nearly dropped the phone. It was one of those moments when you look down on yourself and see how far you've come. It was only two short years ago that I was crying like a baby on my back lawn.

The day of the interview I was excited but totally calm and collected. That is, until Corny called to tell me they were running forty-five minutes behind schedule. That's all it took for me to get very, very nervous. I meditated and ended up having a fantastic conversation with Oprah. We talked about the Law of Attraction, the meetings and about my dream of having a weekly podcast to reach more people.

I had six weeks until the show aired, and in that time I put up the website and started giving teleseminars. Within a few months of the first airing of the interview the podcast was going out to countries all over the world—and that's just *one* of the amazing successes I have manifested in my life since I left my cocoon.

The first part of my story is not unusual. So many women give up walking their own path in order to find a husband and follow him down *his* path! To some extent, all of us—women and men—suffer from what I call the *"Jerry Maguire* Syndrome," wherein we believe that we need someone else to make us feel complete. Is it any wonder we feel lost and devastated if a relationship doesn't work out?

How did I make it through the most difficult time of my life? By giving myself my undivided attention. By focusing on my own healing, by walking my own path. After one transformational year in my cocoon, I knew for sure that I had to complete myself first. When I emerged from my cocoon, I flew. I still cocoon from time to time. It is a gift I give myself in pursuit of my *new* ultimate goal: joy.

Maritza Parra trains and coaches people to use the principles of self-empowerment and easy Internet tools to achieve financial freedom. After being featured on Oprah & Friends: *"The Soul Series," Parra became an expert at creating products quickly via teleseminars, ebooks and video. Known as the "Product Creation Queen" by her fellow online entrepreneurs, Parra teaches people how to create products and market them online from her membership site, www. EasyOnlineMarketingTraining.com, and at the Hacienda, her retreat center in San Antonio, Texas.*

The Eye of the Hurricane

Conrad Drapeau

Picture the world you live in as one huge hurricane. You're stuck; you can't get away from it—ever. A hurricane is a powerful storm accompanied by widespread circular bands of wind, rain, thunder and lightning. It causes a great deal of destruction as it moves along its path. In the middle, the eye of the hurricane, there is an incredibly peaceful space filled with beauty, unaffected by the chaos surrounding it.

Most of us live in the bands of the hurricanes, always stuck in turmoil, moving at a mind-blowing velocity in an unstoppable circular fashion. Most of us experience the "hurricanes" in our lives as destructive, devastating forces, totally unaware of the peace that lives within them, the opportunity for grace, growth and gratitude right at their very center. When faced with crisis, why not choose to live in the eye of the hurricane?

Moments before we received the phone call that would change our lives forever, my wife Carol and I were financially free, believing we were building a legacy for our family, believing our assets and investments were in good hands. They weren't. Turns out we had entrusted our money—our *future*—to unscrupulous people who had nearly wiped out our entire fortune.

"We just lost eighty percent of everything we own." Even though I heard myself tell my wife the news, I couldn't believe what I was saying. We were just getting used to our hard-earned abundance, and then poof! It was gone in the blink of an eye. We were not alone. It's a global problem of epic proportions, and there is no place to hide. Most of us are experiencing the impact of the recent economic crisis. Every day we hear new stories of loss. Jobs, homes, savings and investments are disappearing rapidly, often without warning. Carol and I were the lucky ones— we lost most of it, but we didn't lose it all. Still, at the time it was the biggest challenge of our lives, and we were at a loss as to what to do next.

> *When faced with crisis, why not choose to live in the eye of the hurricane?*

What we needed was a plan, a road map to help us navigate through this unexpected and sudden event. We needed someone who understood what we were going through. After all, a huge financial loss is not something you feel comfortable sharing with your family and friends. In fact, we felt embarrassed and guilty, because we had entrusted our family's future to the wrong people, people who became more than friends, people we loved. All of it was gone in a flash. We should have just given it all away to our family right from the start. I felt sick to my stomach.

Then, one morning after that fateful phone call, I realized I was as well prepared as anyone to tackle this challenge. I was the "someone" we needed to pull us out, over and through to a place of renewed peace. Taking stock, I ran through the various setbacks, disappointments and stumbling blocks I had come up against in my professional life. Truth be told, I've had more than my share of bumps and bruises. The first and most memorable was when, after giving everything to my job as branch manager at an IT company, I was demoted to sales rep. I was shocked. Sure, our numbers were down, but I had a ton of responsibility.

Couldn't the President see how vested I was, how loyal I was to the company?

That first setback sent me into a slump. All my life I had been told to climb high, and still higher up the ladder, and here I was being told my highest level of competence was set at sales rep. My entire self-worth was tied up in my career—my title, my accomplishments and having control. I felt like a failure, defeated and ashamed, so much so that I told everyone it was my decision to go back and focus on sales. My confidence was at an all-time low, and I had the low sales to prove it. After a few months of poor performance, I was given an ultimatum: produce or you're gone.

About that time a friend asked me, "Conrad, are you playing on the court or are you watching from the stands?" I didn't have to answer. We both knew I was sitting in the stands feeling sorry for myself. I decided to face the worst-case scenario—losing my job. What would I do? Get another job. Could I get a new job? Absolutely. Would I lose my possessions? Not likely.

I didn't just hang onto my job; I triumphed. I used a humiliating, depressing experience to transform my performance and up my game. I came out of it a different person, better on so many levels.

Suddenly I realized that even the worst outcome wasn't that bad. This awareness allowed me to step out of my rut, turn off the emotional autopilot, and make a conscious decision to get back in the game. So I took baby steps. Though I didn't have much success in the beginning, I was in motion, and I started feeling better about myself. My instincts resurfaced, and eventually I got some small deals. Since I had nothing to lose, I took on our most challenging prospect, the one nobody could crack. Twelve months after receiving the ultimatum, I was named "Salesman of the Year," breaking through the commission ceiling and earning an unheard-of forty percent of the gross profits from my sales.

I didn't just hang onto my job; I triumphed. I used a humiliating, depressing experience to transform my performance and up my game. I came out of it a different person, better on so many levels. I continued to take on challenges, eventually joining a very risky start-up and helping to take its value from zero to one hundred million in four years. I knew it would be the biggest challenge of my career, but I happily dove in. I had an intuitive inner belief that I could turn this around because every success and failure I had experienced up until that point prepared me for the next big challenge.

Over the years, I discovered powerful techniques to help quiet the mind and achieve inner peace, mental and physical exercises based on Eastern and Western philosophies. Practicing and applying these skills in my daily life gave me a strong foundation, so that when Carol and I were faced with losing almost all of our money, I was able to approach the event with context, perspective and confidence. Within ninety days, we were able to rise up from the depths of despair and establish a new footing. Within this period our entire "space" changed. We sold our home, my wife began taking self-help classes and I was presented with an exciting new job opportunity. Even though the battle with our former accountants and money managers waged on, we had gained control of our lives. We were shaken, but not broken.

We all have our share of difficulties. We all experience storms—sometimes hurricanes—throughout our lives, and we all get caught up in the chaos. The key to surviving unexpected events is to first acknowledge and embrace the reality of your situation, then take control by facing your fears about possible outcomes, and finally take action—in baby steps, if you have to— to generate momentum and empower yourself to thrive. First among these is to embrace the event and declare to yourself, "I don't understand why this is happening, but I'm willing to accept the challenge knowing the lessons learned from this experience are absolutely essential for my growth and evolution."

The approach I followed after my demotion and ultimatum enabled me to transform into a stronger, smarter, more courageous person, and later, when we lost eighty percent of our net worth, I followed a more enlightened version of that approach to regain control and a sense of peace.

If we had not lost the money, I may not have found my true calling in serving others, and I most certainly would not have created an action plan to help other people successfully navigate crisis and turn stressful situations into opportunities for new-found vitality. And if I had not learned how to alchemize the

---

Someone, somewhere is wishing for a clean slate right now; setbacks, bumps and even tragedies give you an automatic clean slate.

---

experience and easily find the peaceful center of chaotic situations, I may not have been able to survive the most devastating unexpected event of my life: the day Carol was diagnosed with an inoperable brain tumor.

Losing a fortune is meaningless compared to losing my sweetheart. Drawing on the skills I developed with every challenge, every bump, every crisis, I was able to navigate this new, terrible hurricane, to take Carol's hand and lead us both to the peaceful eye of our last storm.

Approach every crisis, every stressful situation as an opportunity to reinvent yourself. Someone, somewhere is wishing for a clean slate right now; setbacks, bumps and even tragedies give you an *automatic* clean slate. It's the hidden benefit you can't see when you're bouncing around in the bands, lost in the chaos—the chance to create a new and better world for you.

By embracing and acknowledging the event, by imagining the worst-case scenario and seeing yourself navigate through it, by establishing a plan and taking action on the things you can control, you will pull through any unexpected event or stressful situation. You will survive. And you may even end up living the life you were meant to live.

Conrad Drapeau is the author of the forthcoming book, Inspired To Live Right, *and the founder of Awakening Clarity, a transformational and sustainable program created to help people live inside the peaceful eye of the hurricane regardless of the events and chaos life's dramas bring. After playing a significant role in taking an under-funded technology company with no proven products or a visible market from zero to one hundred million in value in less than four years, Conrad achieved financial freedom and settled into early retirement. Two years later, eighty percent of his total worth vanished, wiped out by people he trusted.*

A successful entrepreneur, Conrad was no stranger to sudden and devastating setbacks. His life and work experience, along with his study of Eastern and Western philosophies, became the basis for the Awakening Clarity framework. These powerful tools proved to be invaluable during difficult times, especially during the final journey with his wife, Carol. Through great loss and difficult life experiences, Conrad discovered his true calling—to guide and inspire people caught up in stress and confusion to a place of infinite inner peace. Join the global movement of people who are "inspired to live right" at www.AwakeningClarity.com.

The Science of Attracting Joy

Angela Bussio

What did you wish for, the last time you found a penny, blew out a birthday candle or spotted the first star in the night sky? Now imagine you have the power to make that wish come true. Would it bring you lasting happiness? Would it bring you joy?

Sometimes the things, experiences and opportunities we think we want cause stress in our lives, because although we may *think* they are what we want, they may not be in our best or highest good. We can't always know whether what we're asking for is something that is good for us. Perhaps you have had the experience of finally getting what you want, then realizing that there were unintended negative consequences—then regretting you ever made that wish.

I learned this the hard way. Several years ago, I experienced a nervous breakdown trying to attract things that were not in my own best and highest good, Everything I thought I had wanted fell in on me at once, and with such negative consequences that I couldn't deal with it. I knew I didn't want to stay in this negative place, this "hell." I could remember a time when I could fly!

As a young girl, most nights I dreamed I was flying. I still have those dreams, and the feeling is extraordinary; being able to will myself off the ground, defy gravity and rise above it all. My quest to experience this exhilaration in my "real," waking life began at age fourteen. In my search, I discovered principles and practices for navigating through life in a way that is, literally, like flying. Key among them was the notion of personal responsibility, that I was really the creator of my experiences. I could choose to be a victim or I could consciously create my life.

Through my study and practice of conscious creation, I learned the power of visualization and setting intention. I learned how to design my life. After discovering these new concepts, I became

---

What transpired in my life as a result of my experiment was as exhilarating as flying. Utilizing the tools of conscious creation, my life became almost magical.

---

excited at the prospect of what I might be able to create. I had learned to set goals for myself in all the different areas of my life: physical, spiritual, intellectual and emotional. I had also learned to ask God to assist me every day, in all that I did. I decided to experiment, combining all of these concepts.

As a teenager I would wake at five o'clock in the morning, exercise, make a spiritual connection, review my written goals and then meditate for twenty minutes, visualizing the day I wanted to create. My goals became kind of a launch pad for the content of my visualization. I would visualize all the different scenarios that might play out in each area of my life in great sensory detail, and then, if there was something in particular that I wanted to happen that day, I concentrated on it and visualized it happening. What transpired in my life as a result of my experiment was as exhilarating as flying. Utilizing the tools of conscious creation, my life became almost magical.

There are too many examples to share in this story, so I will share one of my favorite results. When I was sixteen years old, I really wanted to get out of high school and get on with my life, but I didn't have enough credits to graduate early. At the time, my hero was Barbara Walters. I really wanted a job like hers. By following the conscious creation formula I developed, I got both of my wishes. In the last semester of my junior year, I was selected to be part of a new executive internship program. I was sent to work at a large NBC affiliate radio station in San Francisco, and was able to actually produce and moderate several programs. I received school credit for the experience *and* graduated early!

Decades before the phenomenon of the book and movie *The Secret,* I called my conscious creation experiments "my secret." I believed wholeheartedly that I could achieve anything my heart desired—which I did. By age seventeen, I had manifested a high-salaried job in a field I loved and was driving a hot little sports car.

> *I will tell you that, as soon as I stopped intentionally designing my life and fell asleep at the wheel, my daily miracles ceased. I stopped flying in my dreams and in my life.*

I kept up this practice for several years. It was quite a ride, but I was already beginning to notice that what I wanted sometimes had deleterious consequences! I realized I had discovered a powerful mechanism for consciously creating my life, but that it was a power that should not be taken lightly.

After attracting and marrying one of the greatest men in the universe, I got caught up in the day-to-day realities of mother-hood and sucked into some of the negative drama patterns that can happen to anyone. The daily habits that I had cultivated and practiced for years somehow dropped to the bottom of my list. I will tell you that, as soon as I stopped intentionally designing my life and fell asleep at the wheel, my daily miracles ceased. I stopped flying in my dreams and in my life.

Then, after several years, it happened—my nervous breakdown. I know what it is like to be depressed and anxious, living with the fruits of a negatively focused life. But ultimately, I am grateful for that period of my life. Without it, I would not have learned the powerful lesson of how to liberate myself *from* it.

Remembering the empowered spirit I had in my younger years, I started studying anything and everything that would help me improve my original formula. During this time I graduated with

---

There really is a science to attracting what you want in life, a proven formula for shifting out of old patterns and—if you choose—changing your energy to the frequency of joy.

---

a BS in psychology, and was introduced and to and became a master teacher and practitioner of energy psychology and mind medicine, new brain pattern-shifting techniques anyone can learn that allowed me to really clear out both the conscious and "unconscious" negative patterns that I had formed.

Most importantly, I realized that when I partnered with the "creator of the mechanism"—God—to participate in my conscious creation practice, I could attract what was in my best and highest good more often. I could get my life into a more positive behavior pattern, and raise the frequency and energy of what I was experiencing in my daily life.

I believe that every emotional state has a pattern of behaviors that creates a frequency or energy that attracts experiences of the same frequency. Using this model, I describe "joy" as a frequency that we can only attain as we partner with God. If our thoughts really do create, wouldn't it be powerful to have God's thoughts creating the behavior patterns that would raise our frequency to the level of joy?

Using this paradigm, I have manifested many amazing experiences that bring me closer and closer to this frequency of joy. I experience fewer unwanted consequences, and sometimes some amazing surprises that some would call "miracles." With God as my partner in every wish, my life has started to reflect a divine purpose that benefits not only me, but also everyone around me. I have a new formula that incorporates my newfound knowledge. I have distilled this into a process that I call the "Science of Attracting Joy."

There really is a science to attracting what you want in life, a proven formula for shifting out of old patterns and—if you choose—changing your energy to the frequency of joy. My four-step process, which I call my "Attracting Joy Compass," helps people create more purposeful lives that honor their highest priorities. It is summarized using compass directions as a guiding metaphor for the journey:

- AWARENESS (East): Let the sun come up on new ideas and knowledge, and have a clear picture of how your brain and the world really work.

- VISION (South): In the best light of day, get a clear picture of what you would rather experience; set new intentions.

- CLARITY (West): Let the sun go down on issues that keep you stuck! Clear away negative patterns that make change difficult using powerful energy psychology and mind medicine techniques.

- CONNECTION (True North): Know your destiny. Really make a divine connection to check your desires against what is really in your highest good.

Using this process, I have discovered that every day can really be a journey toward a higher state. It is a journey that never ends—but knowing I have a process for change helps me navigate each day toward a destination of my choosing. I share this with you to give you a glimpse of what could be possible with your own goals.

That last wish you whispered under your breath—you *can* know if it's really what's best for you, and there *is* a way to make it yours. You can learn the scientific formula for attracting all that you want. You have the ability to change your patterns and frequencies to a higher level. Won't you join me on this journey to joy?

———————

Angela Bussio is a master teacher and practitioner of energy psychology and mind medicine techniques. She specializes in establishing new patterns in the brain to foster permanent, real change. A dynamic speaker and life coach, Angela has successfully helped clients and participants learn the practical skills, principles and techniques that foster genuine growth. She holds a BS in psychology and is a certified Master Rapid Eye/Energy Psychology Therapist.

Angela is the author of two forthcoming books: The Science of Attracting Joy, *and the eBook/site,* The 21st Century Guide to Emotional Healing. *She has also been the featured life coach on the television program* Hometeam. *Angela resides in the heart of the Rocky Mountains with her husband and five children. To learn more about Angela, visit www.AngelaBussio.com. To begin your own journey to joy, and join Angela in her "Navigating Time 101" YouTube Challenge, visit www.TheScienceOfAttractingJoy.com.*

The Comeback

Tara Sheahan

I'm a mountain girl: sunburned nose, a great set of lungs, toenails with purple-blue bruises from trail running and a muddy pair of shoes next to the door, wet from criss-crossing Alpine streams. I love climbing misty peaks, running through meadows full of wildflowers, and hooting loudly to hear the echo of my voice bouncing off rock walls far above—none of which seemed possible ten years ago. I am grateful for all of this, for every experience and for all of the people who have come into my life.

I was born in Denver to two hardworking parents who made extraordinary sacrifices for my brother, sister and me to live our dreams. Later we moved to Breckenridge, an old mining town turned ski resort that sits high in the Rocky Mountains. It was here that I first fell in love with skiing—and winning—my eleven year-old body moving so fast through the snow it felt like flying. It is here that I first fell in love with me, my forty-something body broken and battered from two life-threatening illnesses and fighting to heal. And it is here, in these mountains, that I found my way back to my dream.

We moved to Breckenridge to ski. Dad became the mountain manager of the ski resort. We became fixtures on the slopes and in the lodge, wolfing down French fries that fueled us when the snowstorms turned our hands and feet into ice blocks. I skied with my brother Michael and sister Keli, but when the cute boys from out of town showed up, I skied with them! I also started Alpine racing, but after two high-speed crashes I decided I would become a cross-country ski racer.

Our high school was—and still is—home to a top youth Nordic skiing program. When I ski raced, the program was run by a legendary coach named "Giber," and Dave Quinn, his assistant coach. In his early twenties and in remission from cancer, Dave

---

Whenever I felt sad or lonely I went skiing. Flying, surrounded by softly falling snowflakes, feeling the rhythm of my body, I felt peaceful.

---

was one of the first people to talk to me about going for my dreams, and we quickly became best friends. A year after we met, Dave's cancer returned. Within months, he was gone, leaving me with the memory of his beautiful, quiet voice and the belief that I had a special gift to be one of the best skiers in the world.

Within three years, Keli and I made the US Ski Team. Shortly thereafter I went through a traumatic sexual experience that knocked the fight right out of me. My self-esteem plummeted, but I repressed my emotions, which affected my body and caused injuries. Winning races made me feel significant, worthy and loved. Whenever I felt sad or lonely I went skiing. Flying, surrounded by softly falling snowflakes, feeling the rhythm of my body, I felt peaceful.

Recruited by Middlebury College, which had the best ski team in the country at the time, I set a goal—*the goal*—of winning a gold medal in the Winter Olympic games. It was the ultimate dream, and although I knew I could do it, I was also afraid to fail. So I trained even harder, pushing my body to go faster, faster, faster. While I was at Middlebury our ski team won two NCAA championships, and I earned a two-sport All-American title (in cross country running and skiing). I had great times in college. Still, even the wins in the external world couldn't heal my inner world.

After my last college race, I put my dream away in a little corner of my heart and left competitive skiing behind. I moved to New York, and put my experience to use as a public relations account executive for sports and consumer product companies. When I married my husband Casey in 1988, I was a vice president at Inclyne Sports, a pioneer in packaging sports television programs. After we started a family, we moved to Oregon, and later Vermont, for Casey's work. I gave up my professional life to be present for our two sons.

In 1995 I blew out my knee skiing in Breckenridge while visiting my parents. After undergoing reconstructive surgery, I started experiencing a lot of pain in my forearms and knees, and later throughout my whole body. My hair started falling out. The pain was so excruciating, I could barely brush my teeth. I forgot the basic facts of my life—where I lived, the names of my family members, my phone number. None of the eight doctors

---

I surrendered to the Creator and said, "I just want to watch my children grow up. I just want to be."

I consulted could figure out what was wrong with me because I didn't "look sick." But I knew I was dying. I heard a voice inside me say, "If you stop moving, you'll die," so every day I walked, even if it was just a quarter mile down our country road. Sometimes it was too much and I would just lie on the ground.

I surrendered to the Creator and said, "I just want to watch my children grow up. I just want to be." After this affirmation of letting go and giving myself over to something greater than myself, I experienced a "burst" of healing, and began a spiritual journey toward wellness. Stripped of all my labels and everything I believed made me significant—great cook, super parent, athlete—there was nothing left but me. Just me. I began to clear my emotional blocks, and with every letting go I felt more energy return to my body. My illness forced me to slow down for the first time in my life, which turned out to be a massive gift because I was able to connect with the transformational power of nature. And in nature I came to know the Creator—not the domineering, threatening presence I feared growing up Catholic, but a loving, benevolent, beautiful Creator that was not separate from me, but *in me.*

We moved back to Colorado to be closer to my parents, and it was there that I finally received my diagnosis of Lyme disease. I sought treatment from wonderful western and alternative medicine doctors, and continued my spiritual discovery. I put myself first, and in doing so, I was able to reconstruct my life and help heal my body. As an athlete, I was hardwired to see the connection between the emotional and the physical, and I continued to notice the direct correlation between letting go of emotions and getting better.

It took three years, but I beat it. However, my six-year adventure with illness was only half-done. Not long after I recovered fully from Lyme disease, I developed a grapefruit-sized ovarian tumor that grew onto my colon and irritated my intestinal valve. Again, it was a difficult illness that prevented me from doing the basics, like eating. But I was better prepared this time. This time, I knew intuitively I would survive.

One year later my tumor was surgically removed, and I began working with a therapist to attend to the long-festering wounds that had plagued me since high school. In excellent health and able to run pain-free, I attended the Winter Olympics in Salt Lake City with my family. Serendipitously, we could only get tickets to cross country events. Mesmerized by the racers, glued to their every graceful, powerful move, I suddenly realized I was crying. "I have to finish this," I said to Casey, and just like that I brought my dream out into the light of day. I set my sights on the 2006 Winter Olympics in Turin, Italy, and began training. I was forty-two years old.

Making my big comeback was easier than I thought it would be. I was much stronger emotionally than I had been the first time around, and it didn't take long to get into shape. I trained twice a day, lifted weights and competed with the best skiers in the country, women in their teens and early twenties. I often placed in the top ten, and was listed as an Olympic hopeful. When I finished a race I felt so grateful that my body, once broken, was able to fly. It was such a gift.

How did I do it? How did I survive two life-threatening illnesses and come back to compete and win races against women less than half my age? I was competing in joy, the mountain girl in her element—embracing sport as a playground, not a battleground.

I set my sights on the 2006 Winter Olympics in Turin, Italy, and began training. I was forty-two years old.

Illness was my pathway to higher consciousness, and that difficult yet soul-awakening adventure freed me from the confines of ego. I no longer derived worth from winning, which ironically moved me closer to my goal of winning a gold medal.

Two months before the Olympic tryouts, however, I stepped on a rattlesnake while training on a run in Salida, Colorado, and the snake bit my ankle. Looking at my swollen leg in the emergency room the next morning, I knew my Olympic dream was over. I laughed, because I knew that my training was meant for some greater journey. A few months later, I learned Native Americans believe that when a rattlesnake bites you, you die and are reborn. I began to understand how I was moving away from the ego-driven aspect of competitive sports, toward a heart-centered life.

It may not feel like it at the time—in fact, it most definitely will *not* feel like it at the time, not at first—but chronic illness truly is a path to awakening to your highest potential. It is calling on you to pay attention to your inner world, and to discover a relationship with the Creator, a universal energy that is your best friend 24/7! In illness, you are stripped of all that you believe makes you who you are; you are left bare so that you can choose *you*. In choosing you, you heal yourself. When you are healed, you too can pull your own dream out from the cobwebbed corners of your heart and go for it, no matter the circumstances.

Today I run for the pure joy of it; today I ski with heart. Some may say that I never pulled off my comeback, but I would disagree. You see, I wasn't just coming back as a championship skier bound for the Olympics, and I wasn't just coming back from near-fatal illnesses. I was coming back to the divine in me.

Tara Sheahan is a motivational speaker, meditation teacher and life coach, and a partner in All Energy TV, a global Internet and iPhone media company reporting on positive world events. Tara's experience as a competitive athlete and her recovery from life-threatening illness inform her motivational life teachings, inspiring people to "action their brilliance" by becoming aware of the inner world and the destructive emotional patterns and conditions that cause "dis-ease" and suffering. She is a graduate of the Oneness University Process (Level 1 and Level 2), and is trained to give Oneness Blessings, a non-denominational experience that initiates a neurobiological change in the brain resulting in a growth in consciousness.

Tara was a member of the US Cross Country Ski Team, won two national championships and was Middlebury College's first two-sport All-American title winner (in cross country running and skiing). After an absence of more than twenty years, she returned to competitive skiing and raced for the Subaru Factory Team and the Fischer Team in her pursuit to make the Winter Olympic Team. Tara thanks Casey, her husband of over twenty years; her two boys, Aidan and Caelin; her Mom, Dad, family and friends; all her healers, teachers, and coaches; and the profound wisdom the divine sent to her via each and every person in her life. To learn more about Tara, visit www.TaraSheahan.com.

Self Love:
The Key to Authenticity

Marcy Neumann

The key to health, happiness and every kind of success lies in identifying, connecting with and loving your true self. What this requires is listening to the urgings of your spirit and taking some action that supports it. If you are in search of an authentic life, look no further: listen, and love.

The sustained, deep sense of happiness, fulfillment and authenticity I know and trust these days was not always with me. Its beginnings, rather, can be at least partly traced to an epiphany I had in the summer of 2002, while I was attending a relative's wedding.

I was living an idyllic life at the time; perfect, many would say. I had four beautiful children, a loving husband, a great job, big house, lots of friends, vacation homes, fancy cars—you name it. My life had the outward appearance of what seemed to be a very healthy success based on spirituality and values I cherished; I was a Reiki Master and a vegetarian with a daily spiritual practice; I was an affluent woman with a happy family. I thought I had it all! Sometimes, though, I would find myself filled with a feeling of emptiness or loneliness. Persistent health problems had begun to plague me; at fifty, arthritis, constant headaches, digestive issues and even nocturnal panic attacks had become severe and intrusive.

The relative hosting the pre-wedding party had a tipi in her back yard. I was so drawn to it that I sneaked out of the party and crawled inside the tipi. When I pulled back the flaps and looked up at the stars, I was awestruck by their beauty and brilliance. They seemed to reach out to me. I lay on my back, staring up at them and thinking about how lucky I was, how grateful for my perfect life. Suddenly, like ticker tape across my mind's eye, ran the question, "How much longer do I have to do this, Lord?"

I was so shocked that I broke out in a cold sweat, sprang up and out of the tipi, and vomited in the bushes. My heart seemed to be thumping out of my chest. I couldn't imagine where on earth that thought had come from! Then I realized that I must be repressing some deep, genuine unhappiness, and I decided to tackle the job of unraveling it. As I did, chaos struck, and my "perfect" life unraveled too. But wonderfully, remarkably, my spirit rose to the surface from the subterranean depths where it had been hiding for many, many years.

Once I began to see the big picture—not just what I wanted to see—I realized that my spirit had been dying; my "perfect life" had been a façade. It had been expressed through physical manifestations. Realizing my marriage was as crippling as the arthritis in my hips, I told my husband that I wanted a divorce. He was shocked; everyone was shocked. We were the "perfect" couple, the "perfect" family. I walked away from everything that had defined me for nearly thirty years in order to recreate my life. With professional help, I identified my fears and worked through them, following the guidance and urgings of my spirit. Miraculously, one by one, my physical ailments disappeared.

Before, my self-love had been limited. Doses of self-care and bursts of authenticity were like bandages that placated me and allowed me to stay in the old life; they gave me little nibbles of what I needed to stay sane and connected. During the tipi epiphany, however, I allowed my spirit to come forward and say, "Who are you kidding? You're living an inauthentic life, and you're miserable." I was living from event to event, reacting. I was looking for those events to keep me distracted. From what? An existence in which my spirit is in charge and determines every aspect of my life. That is the life I lead now, and the life I—and all of us—have always been meant to lead.

I started to analyze what I had actually done, which was to claim this process of loving myself. As I started to put myself first and let my spirit guide me to what was good—or not good— for

---

If you are in search of an authentic life, look no further: listen, and love.

---

me based upon how I was feeling, I had healed and empowered myself. What an amazing affirmation of my spirit, self and decisions! My life's work became empowering other people to listen to their deepest feelings, follow the voices of their spirits and love themselves.

In awe of the effects of the changes I was making in my own life, I was inspired to write a manual incorporating Reiki for a self-healing course called CELLpH LOVE. The premise, based on an integration of scientific and spiritual healing principles, is that our every thought and feeling inform and affect every cell in our bodies. Bringing the characteristics of love—such as compassion, respect and kindness—to ourselves, we can actually shift the pH of our cells, awakening memory of cellular health. pH balance is a prime indicator of health; it is the platform for cellular reproduction. Loving ourselves is the key to health and happiness!

Self-love is an act of bravery, because it requires that you live through your eyes only. We're programmed, from our earliest moments in life, to react and respond as others want us to. We're in the crib, and we're crying—and the first time mom doesn't come running, we think, "What did I do wrong?" "Am I unlovable?" It begins that early. We adjust our behavior to please others in the hope they'll give us the love we want.

We are thinking and feeling beings, and every single experience creates feelings. Those feelings create thoughts—and those thoughts create our reality. Our realities are based on behavior we have created in hopes of pleasing others, rather

---

Ask yourself, "Is this choice I am making in support of my spirit?"

---

than the urgings of our spirits. When we simply follow those urgings, we realize how much of our lives we're living through other people's eyes, giving away our power of creation! We're not meant to sacrifice that. We are obligated, rather, to explore every aspect of our being. It's our uniqueness, not our programming, that is the jigsaw puzzle piece needed to complete the Universal picture.

This work requires a creation of consciousness in which you are aware of what you feel each moment, and act accordingly. Look at what you're feeling and where it's coming from and, in that very moment, love yourself. Regardless. Be a true friend to yourself.

Speak to yourself as you would to a good friend. Know that you did the best you could at that moment. Maybe you can do it differently the next time! Self-love means bringing the same kindness to yourself that you would to another person.

As you focus on being conscious of how you're feeling, each moment bridges to the next, and the next—until it becomes a way of life. Then, if you're feeling out of balance, you will recognize and attend to it immediately, instead of sweeping it under the rug. If I'm feeling resentful, I stop right then and there and ask, "Are my thoughts going in the direction of my greatest good?" If I need to change my thoughts, I do so, and thus I am changing the effects of those emotions on my whole being.

For many of us, thoughts are like a drive down a familiar street. We're so engrossed in our inner conversation, we lose sight of where it's taking us. It could be the exact opposite direction of where we want to go! I say, "Divert your gaze!" Pull that car over until you get your thoughts moving in a direction that will create enough energy to support your every goal. This is the power of the Law of Attraction! Ask yourself, "Is this choice I am making in support of my spirit?"

Over the years, the more I cultivated this consciousness and learned to trust the urgings of my spirit, the more energy, creativity and inspiration flowed through me. I was constantly dreaming up products like Create UR Dreams, a vision board kit that brings people's hopes and dreams to fruition. In 2007, with no business plan or experience, I rented an office and started my business. Because of the trust I had developed in my own process,

---

Look at what you're feeling and where it's coming from and, in that very moment, love yourself. Regardless. Be a true friend to yourself.

I felt free to disregard the many naysayers. Instead I cocooned in self-love and trust, knowing I was truly serving the universe.

Incorporating the very principles my products were designed to utilize and ignite, my God-sent assistant and I had our products on the shelf within five months! I had no business know-how and she had no product development experience. But we used the guiding principles I speak of to attract the outsourcing we needed and bring the business forward. When progress faltered, I asked myself, "What inside of me needs to be changed?"

We won "Best of Show" at an international trade show. Today, thousands of people are using our products for their personal and business manifestations. J. Lopez Motherway, the Long Island publisher of *Natural Awakenings*, uses her Create UR Dream board kit to grow her new business. In one month, she tripled her sales, and a year later her magazine had grown faster than in any other territory in the organization! This is just one of countless examples of how self-love, spirit guidance and Law of Attraction principles heal our lives and propel us forward.

I keep my goals alive by continuing to do my own personal work. This allows me to control my thoughts, and our lives are a mirror of our ability to do that. Believing and receiving are inextricably linked. Believe that you are loved and supported by this universal force and receive evidence in every aspect of your life!

Marcy Neumann is an RN, spiritual minister, Reiki master, hypnotist, Law of Attraction expert and the creator of the scientifically based, cutting-edge CELLpH (Self) Love program. Her company, Heartlites Inc., is a leading manufacturer of personal and spiritual development products such as Create UR Mate and Create UR Dreams. The Law of Attraction principles have become the basis of her Resistance Identification Program, her very successful consulting practice and her Law of Attraction products and programs. Marcy has helped hundreds of individuals, businesses and organizations to flourish and achieve great success. For more information about Marcy, to find seminar dates or to purchase Heartlites products, visit www.heartlitesinc.com.

Stay in the Ring

Chris Howard

Fifteen years ago, I made a decision that changed everything for me. I committed to one single purpose: to teach people how to make their lives better. Up until that point I had lived a life familiar to most people, a life of fits and starts. I'd worked in the hotel resort industry, but stopped before I became general manager. I'd studied martial arts and attained my black belt, but then stopped for a while. There were other things too, things I took on simultaneously, looking for that perfect combination, hoping something would take hold and catch fire.

One day, while sitting in my little converted garage, I read a passage in Napoleon Hill's *Think and Grow Rich* that really resonated with me. He talked about how important single-mindedness of purpose was for creating a huge fortune. Right away, I got that the same rule applied no matter what I wanted to achieve, and I made the decision to commit to one path and stay the course no matter what unexpected turns I encountered along the way. So I committed to my soul's purpose of teaching people how to change their lives for the better, and embarked on the best career path to achieve my purpose, public speaking. Although I had no education other than life experience, I hatched the dream of becoming a nationally known public speaker and media personality with my own training company. I set a twofold goal of earning one million dollars in one year and speaking all over the United States.

That was the biggest, most impossible dream I could dream back then. I just couldn't fathom anything bigger or better. Although I didn't reach my goal in one year, I kept at it, totally focused on my one, single purpose. The attitude and mindset I learned from martial arts kept me going; that mindset is as important to me as anything I've ever learned from any other form of personal development. It's that warrior spirit—you fall down four times, you get up five—and it's the key to making the impossible possible.

If you're going to have single-mindedness of purpose, you need that spirit, that heart, that willingness to get back up, because the world can beat the crap out of you, especially if you take a chance on your dream. It's like cultivating the Rocky Balboa mentality. You have to come out saying, "One more round, two more rounds, come on! Bring it on!" You have to keep going and you have to keep getting up, no matter what. It's much easier to find that spirit within when you are committed to making your life the expression of your soul's purpose, because anything less than that will tap your energy, and you'll never make it past the first few rounds.

People often get involved in little side businesses so they can make money to one day fuel their dreams, but because they're focused solely on making money, and because they aren't actually working toward their dream, they never make much money at all. You need passion for your single purpose, or you'll never reach your goals. You can't win the fight if you have to leave the ring to sell tickets and souvenirs!

Don't be fooled by the lure of easy money—you'll make five times, ten times, one hundred times the money following your "heart" path than you would by following the "money" path. As Warren Buffet says, "Life is like a snowball. The important thing is finding wet snow and a really long hill." Your "wet snow" is that thing you were born to do, and the "long hill" is being of single-minded purpose—concentrating your efforts on getting that snowball down the hill. The greatest fortunes in the world today were not made from a diversification of focus; they were made from a concentration of focus. Warren Buffet's company, Berkshire Hathaway, was made from a concentration of energy.

Don't be fooled by the lure of easy money—you'll make five times, ten times, one hundred times the money following your "heart" path than you would by following the "money" path.

So were Microsoft, Apple and Virgin Atlantic Airways. Name any hugely successful company and I guarantee there was a total concentration of focus, energy and attention on one purpose behind that success.

The key to getting rich financially, as well as the key to having an emotionally textured, rich life, is to have concentration of focus and energy on what you were born to do, making your life an expression of your soul's purpose and all it was really meant to be. When you are rich in the moment, every moment of every day is spent in the embrace of God, and every moment leads to great tipping points in which you learn to monetize all that you have into ever-expanding wealth. That's where you get really rich. You don't earn one million dollars and call it a day. If you stay the course and learn to monetize well, there are no limitations to your dreams. The impossible becomes possible, you can't dream new dreams fast enough, and that which was unimaginable suddenly becomes part of your everyday life. And that's exactly what happened to me.

In pursuit of my goal, I invested a lot in learning about my industry. I studied for years, worked for four different personal development companies, and was well placed before I ventured out on my own. Still focused on my one singular, soul purpose, I launched my own company nine years ago, and something interesting happened. Everything suddenly tipped and my business exploded.

In his book, *The Tipping Point,* Malcolm Gladwell explains how fax machines became a necessary machine for nearly every business in the Western world. When fax machines first became available, there weren't enough businesses using them to make them worth the purchase price—after all, why would you need a fax machine if none of your customers or vendors had one? But at some point, enough businesses had fax machines, and a tipping point was reached where everyone had to have one in order to do business. That's when fax machines sales went crazy overnight. Not doubled. Not tripled. Sales went completely through the roof almost immediately.

As a result of my single-minded purpose, my business reached a tipping point, and suddenly amazing opportunities hit, hit, hit, one right after another. All of a sudden, everybody knew who I was. All of sudden, we expanded out of the U.S. market. All of a sudden, we were the biggest personal and professional development company in Australia, bigger than many of the star-name speakers that have been around for years. And then, all of a sudden, my peers in the industry knew who I was, and we did twenty-two million dollars in global sales.

Richard Branson said, when he was building Virgin Atlantic, that it's always a struggle to survive. The truth is, there are a lot of ups and downs, loads of unexpected events, twists and turns and plenty of moments when it looks as though you will most certainly fail. You've got to persevere through those moments, because every one of them is an opportunity to grow. And it's the warrior spirit that will embolden you to push on, fueled by your passion, your one true purpose.

Training in martial arts, I experienced several make-or-break moments. When I tested for my black belt, I had to fight everyone in the class until I could no longer hold my hands up. I was getting beaten into a corner, but I still had to find the will to survive.

Somehow I would find it, the heart, and I would get back up. And it's that same spirit that's kept me going in business. The Japanese call it bushido, the warrior spirit to keep moving forward.

Single-minded purpose empowers you to step up and overcome challenges, to face obstacles head on and get around them, over them, through them, whatever it takes to *keep moving forward*.

The Japanese call it bushido, *the warrior spirit to keep moving forward.*

When you overcome a problem, your *bushido* expands, and you are able to take on the next one, and the next one, and the next one. You can go endless rounds in the ring, stay the course as long as it takes, until fortune finally tips in your favor. Because it will tip, of that I am certain.

I never wanted to become an entrepreneur; I just wanted to change the world. But I had to learn business in order to put the structure underneath my dreams. I knew that if I learned how to help other people change their lives for the better, I would also change my own life in the process. So I've made this my lifetime study, my purpose, and it hasn't had a ripple effect of change— it's been a *tidal wave* of change.

Yes, you can be, do, have and create anything you want, but you have to be willing to do what it takes, within ethical guidelines. Pour your energy into a singular direction, concentrate way more energy than the average person would be willing to—that's what makes somebody extraordinary. Success is a lifetime thing; it's the marathon of your life, and as long as you're pointed in the right direction and taking efficient and effective action, as long as you get coaching and feedback along the way, you'll produce extraordinary results. Your steadfast efforts will reach a tipping point where the impossible becomes possible.

Stay in the ring!

Internationally acclaimed lifestyle and wealth strategist Christopher Howard is a best-selling author, a prominent speaker and the owner of Christopher Howard Training. For almost two decades, Chris has researched the success strategies of the world's greatest business, philanthropic and spiritual minds. His extensive knowledge is shared through his books, home study courses and public seminars worldwide. As a result, Chris Howard has helped hundreds of thousands of individuals create the wealth and engineer the lifestyle they truly desire. With operations in the United States, Australia, England, Ireland, New Zealand, China and further expansion scheduled for Europe, Canada and South East Asia, Christopher Howard Training has become one of the fastest-growing personal development training companies in the world.

As a social entrepreneur, Chris Howard has made a philanthropic impact in developing nations worldwide. His endeavors include building a high school in the Huilloq Community in Peru, where previously education stopped after the primary school level. He brought a group of thirty coaches and mentors to work with hundreds of students at CIDA, the first free university in South Africa supported by people like Oprah, Nelson Mandela and Richard Branson. In Cambodia, Chris helps raise awareness for the campaigns of social enterprise Friends International by sharing their messages throughout his global networks. In addition to his own contributions to the Lotus Children's Centre in Mongolia, Chris also continues to share information about their sponsor-a-child campaign so others can follow.

Chris is also a master faculty member of Humanity Unites Brilliance (HUB), an organization committed to making poverty history by creating opportunities through hundreds of millions of micro-loans. Chris travels the world extensively with his wife, Lauren, as they share the gift of transformation through education and entrepreneurial means. To learn more about Chris, visit www.ChrisHoward.com.

Dreams Do Come True

Paula Knudsen

W e've all heard that "it takes a village to raise a child." I believe it also takes a village to make a dream come true. It takes a village to keep a dream growing until it touches everyone and encompasses everything it possibly can.

Dreams are such a powerful force in my life. Whether they are waking ones, in which I brainstorm ways to help make a difference in the world, or whether they come to me as I sleep—full of art, poetry and solutions to problems plaguing friends—dreams have always directed my actions—and in very positive ways for which I will forever be grateful. Who are we without our dreams? We *all* have dreams. And I know from firsthand experience that we are all called to help each other's dreams come to fruition.

Growing up in a wealthy town, I noticed at a very young age that despite the prosperity there, people in my town were still going hungry. I couldn't understand it. How, when so many had so much, could some have so little? It was absurd. I learned that life isn't fair. And I felt stirrings, then, that later led me to pursue a lifelong dream of creating a sustainable end to hunger on the planet.

After hearing Lyn Twist speak about The Hunger Project, I started following my dream by forming a 501(c)(3) organization that created and worked with various anti-hunger projects—

such as Fair Foods, which involved homeless folks in the sale and distribution of donated foods at dollar-bag sites throughout the city of Boston. I organized small food drives in my town. Soon I had involved my local post office in a food drive that ultimately became May's National Food Drive at post offices around the country. Along with friends, volunteers and family members, we delivered donated food to shelters in the Boston area.

Sometimes the nonprofit work was tiring—but it was always rewarding. Thanks to my team, the dream continued to feed itself with more and more action, inspiration and the immeasurably great feeling of making a real difference in the world. It wasn't abstract: the difference was tangible and beautiful.

One day my mother and I, en route to a shelter in Brockton, Massachusetts, picked up a wonderful donation from a bakery: a beautiful yellow cake decorated with pretty curlicues of frosting

---

Generosity creates serendipity.

---

and a little ballerina on top. When we pulled up at the shelter with our load of donations, we saw a little girl in mismatched socks sitting on the front steps, sobbing her heart out. I went to her and asked, "What's wrong, sweetie?" Her sadness was so acute I felt like crying myself. Nose running, she hiccupped, "It's my birthday, and I don't even have a cake!"

My mother and I looked at each other. "Oh my God," I said. "That's why we're here!" We ran in to speak to the director of the shelter, who shortly managed to gather everyone together to sing "Happy Birthday" and present Olivia with her ballerina birthday cake. When I saw the look of surprise and delight on Olivia's face, it made every moment of hard work worthwhile. It's why I did what I did. Generosity creates serendipity.

My work began to yield speaking engagements, not just locally but all over the world. I was invited to Australia to speak about the possibility of a sustainable end to hunger! I spoke at Earth Day in Boston and collected food there, too. I persuaded Aerosmith to make their New Year's Eve concert a food drive for the Boston Food Bank, and I spoke at every opportunity to enroll businesses and organizations as participants. My invitation was simple: each time a meeting, workshop, fundraiser or gathering of any kind occurred, they would simply ask each attendee to bring food items to be contributed to someone else.

In the meantime, my boss at my bartending job was becoming frustrated with my constant need for time off. I didn't know how to juggle all my new responsibilities along with my job, and being a single mom didn't make it any easier. So I got on my knees and asked for a dream. I dreamt THE FRUMPLE FACTORY®. In my dream, my son and his buddies were jumping around on stick horses and yelling, "FRUMPLE, FRUMPLE, FRUMPLE!" In the background, a reel-to-reel of little faces in fairy dust spoke this poem over and over:

> *A FRUMPLE is a little friend, made with love and out of clay.*
> *A FRUMPLE has a goofy face to help you smile all day.*
> *A FRUMPLE in your pocket, or near your bed at night,*
>   *Will help to make things better even if kept out of sight.*
> *Miracles can happen—we know this to be true—*
> *When you hold your FRUMPLE in your hand and whisper*
>   *"I love you."*

I woke up and immediately wrote the dream down. It was the asked-for dream, so complete—and yet so mysterious! Later that day I called my sister to tell her about it. She asked, "Have you made anything yet?" "No," I replied. "Well, get out in the studio and make something," she said. I went directly to my clay studio and started to play. Taking the words of my dream as my inspiration, I started molding funny faces. At first they were big and clunky, and I didn't know what to do with them. Then

I thought perhaps I should make them as necklaces. Soon, I was making thousands of FRUMPLES!

Every night I dreamt a new FRUMPLE poem and wrote it down in the morning. After a hundred nights, I had a hundred poems! I would put a bowl of FRUMPLES out at an event and people could choose their own one-of-a-kind funny face and a poem to go with it. There was a teacher poem, a mom poem, a get-well-soon poem—a poem for everything. Then a doctor approached me and said his son had a machine that could raise the frequency

---

Believe it, dreams do come true. Most people just erase their dreams when they wake up, not stopping to consider their power. Listen to them.

---

of the clay to help balance and focus people. At the time, I laughed at this zany idea. But that's when FRUMPLES really took off—because it worked. And the serendipity started showing up, big time. Right after we started raising the frequency of the FRUMPLES, my friend Richard took one home with him. The next day, he returned with a check and said, "Quit your job and make it happen." I've since paid him back, and he now owns stock in the company.

I've received happy letters from all over the world describing how FRUMPLES have helped people with everything from autism to vertigo. FRUMPLES, as the first dream poem goes, really do make people smile. Each individual FRUMPLE has its own charm and character, as well as its special balancing effects. I now go to shows every weekend and sell these very affordable magical faces and unique designs to every kind of person you can imagine. And while I'm doing it, I connect with them and share my vision of sustainability and making a difference. People walk away inspired to take action.

THE FRUMPLE FACTORY, INC. is the answer to my prayer, a dream come true. It's an honor to create something that supports me as a single mom, and makes a positive change on the planet. Believe it, dreams do come true. Most people just erase their dreams when they wake up, not stopping to consider their power. *Listen* to them.

Keep a dream journal. This is one of the best things you can do for yourself, because the guidance in sleeping dreams is real. A dream from six years ago may tie in with what you want in your life now. With a dream journal, instead of saying, "I wish I'd known this before," you will have paid attention to what has always been coming through you.

It's not hard to do this, or to remember your dreams. Here's what I do: before I go to bed, I drink half a glass of water and repeat ten times, "I will remember my dreams after finishing this water

---

How many people do you need to help in order to make your own dream come true?

---

in the morning." Keep the glass by the side of the bed, with your dream journal and a pen, and when you wake up, drink the rest of the water. It will act as a trigger, and you'll start to remember your dreams. I write down whatever comes to me, even if it's only one word. That's how I got the FRUMPLES and their poems!

Everyone has access to the guidance in their dreams. But not everyone is willing to listen and take action. People say, "I pray all the time." Wonderful! You've got to pray and beat your feet. And you've got to stay open. The people you help will help you. It's not about me—it's about us.

Someone once posed a question to me that lit up every cell in my body. As we talked about next steps for the FRUMPLES, my friend asked, "Paula, if this is what you need next for your business, how many people do you need to help?" What a great question! Now, the first thing I do every morning is look in the mirror and ask myself, "Who can I help today and how can I make a difference in the world?"

Dreams Do Come True

As far I'm concerned, service to the planet is all there is—and we all make a difference. How many people do you need to help in order to make your own dream come true?

Paula Knudsen's heart passion led her to form a 501(c)(3) organization in mere weeks; initiate the National Food Drive with the US Post Office and create THE FRUMPLE FACTORY, INC® to support her humanitarian projects and those of HUB (Humanity Unites Brilliance), a global community of like-minded individuals committed to creating opportunity, sustainability and positive change. Paula has taught and spoken out about the possibility of a sustainable end to hunger in cities all over the world, and has been featured in The Boston Globe, Family Circle, New Age Journal, The New York Times *and in many other print, radio and TV venues, including Liz Walker's news program (where Paula was honored with Liz Walker's Angel Award). She also won a Boston Parent Advocate Award and acknowledgment from the Massachusetts House of Representatives for her work toward a sustainable end to hunger. See the FRUMPLES! Visit www.BlessedBlast.com and www.Frumples. HubHub.org.*

FRUMPLE poem © 1998 Paula Knudsen

Set Your Life on Fire

Linda Christensen, PhD

I believe that however we search for fulfillment—whether it is through travel, spirituality, personal growth, work or any other of the myriad human paths to happiness—the essence of the human quest is to live life to the max. To be able to die without any regrets, knowing we really showed up and gave life our best shot. After years of studying and teaching comparative religion, I think that's what people are searching for in their spiritual quest. The longing for God and enlightenment is a longing for total aliveness. The fire of the spirit is the fire that ignites a life full of passion and joy, and it is that spirit that we all need to resurrect in order to find happiness.

Life doesn't always turn out the way we want. We experience tragedies, broken dreams, financial and career struggles and failed relationships. Many of us are walking around with spirits doused by despair, unable to see what a tremendous gift our lives really are. For many years, I was one of those people—dead without the spirit-given breath of life. Ultimately, I found a way to lift myself from two decades of despair and not just live again but set my life on fire.

I was married for twenty-four years to a man I loved but was unhappy with. My low self-worth supported a kind of passivity; I accepted a lifestyle I didn't want and followed my reclusive husband's wishes over and above my own. I chose to tolerate a lot of misery in my life; my values were such that I was committed to my marriage no matter what, and I confused unconditional love with a conditional relationship.

Though I was always a social creature, my husband was not. So for years we lived in a small, isolated shack on an Indian reservation that had no heat except for a woodstove. In an environment of both material and emotional deprivation, I had to work so hard just to keep warm! I felt so alone and isolated in my home and in my relationship that by the fifth year of my marriage I began to sink into a black hole of despair.

And I was perpetually chopping wood, keeping the fire stoked, scraping ice off the insides of the windows and picking slivers out of my hands. The wood was always wet, and though we tried to dry it before we burned it, it smoked up the small space like a manifestation of the sadness that hung over my head. I had always wanted children, but my husband did not. I once, by fluke, got pregnant. My husband was in such despair

I had this idea that I could become a saint and live in bliss no matter how toxic my environment was.

I thought he might commit suicide. I ended up losing the baby. So we didn't make a family. I used to walk down the street and look in other people's windows wishing I could be like them— surrounded by the warmth of friends and family, eating and laughing, living in a normal house like normal people.

After many years, my husband finally agreed to have a child together, and I gave birth to my beloved son at the age of forty-two. I thought that having a child would help bring us together, but instead it highlighted the differences between my husband and me. More and more, I was going one way and my husband was going the other.

Linda Christensen

I had started to pursue personal growth work, but in the beginning I still held to a certain ideal that got in my way: I thought that if I was not happy, I was the problem. I thought that I should be able to transcend any situation, be so unconditionally loving that I could and should be happy anywhere and in relation to anyone—if I were only big enough, spiritual enough.

I had this idea that I could become a saint and live in bliss no matter how toxic my environment was. This approach only prolonged my misery and despair. In the meantime, however,

---

I decided to love myself, and it was amazing, right away.

I spent a lot of time crying, praying, reading and learning new ways of thinking and being. I was gathering strength, stoking my inner fire in preparation for an actual life. A shamanic journey brought me to the Land of Desolation, where I could leave behind every part of my life and self-image that was dead. I left my marriage there.

I had hated my life for years, but I knew that if I were to survive, I had to get myself to a place where I could embrace it. I had to honor myself first, not second. My spiritual background had taught me that life was all about sacrificing oneself for others in the name of love. It wasn't working. The real turning point came when I made a conscious commitment to myself. It was triggered by a dream. In it, a single-breasted woman leapt toward me from the depths of a lake, raging because of her missing piece. I realized that my womanhood had been stolen, and I had to reclaim not only it but also the fire of my spirit and my whole life. I had to start saying, "Yes!" to me, my life, my spirit and my power.

I then began to *consciously create* a space around myself that would only let good things in. And because I changed my beliefs about myself, I accepted the inevitable: I had to leave my marriage. Leaving that toxic environment made all the difference. I couldn't reap the fruit of all the work I had done on myself until I made that step. Certain energetic bonds and ties can hurt us rather than help us and need to be severed.

I decided to love myself, and it was amazing, right away. Before, the only time I could feel that kind of joy was when I was alone in nature. Now I feel the fire of my spirit has ignited my whole life with joy and passion, love and curiosity.

Of course, all this is a process. Making a commitment to yourself isn't like a snap of the fingers. You have to do it consciously, and on a daily basis. You have to practice holding your ground in the face of others' desires, judgments, needs and threats. The more you do it the easier it gets—and there's no way around this step. Only after you make a commitment to yourself can you begin to love yourself.

Love is the key. When you love yourself, you're able to fall in love with life. Your passion brings you joy. You enjoy yourself and your own company. What you're enjoying is your core self. And when you're connected with your core self, you can find your purpose and live what is to you your best, ultimate life. Setting your life on fire means falling in love with it. When you do, life becomes sacred, holy and precious.

How to open to love? Heal your heart. Don't be afraid to feel your feelings. To be fully alive, you need to be a fully feeling person. Smell the air, listen to the birds singing: awakening your senses and your emotions will awaken your passion. Being fully able to feel means you can be compassionate with yourself and others, unafraid of pain and yet not sinking or rolling in it. Just allow yourself to go there, be present and then journey through to the other side.

Embrace and accept the tides of life: enter into its difficulties without creating a self-pitying story. There are others who experience pain; life has not singled you out for misery. Working in a group can help put this into perspective. Try finding people like yourself who want to set their lives on fire, and see how you can help each other through mutual coaching, accountability and support when you lose hope. An authentic supporter will never tell you to just "get over it." The people who will help you as you do the great work of reclaiming your spirit will let you feel and be exactly who you are.

These days, for me, it doesn't matter where I am or what I'm doing, I enjoy my own company and the company of others. I

> *If I don't have exactly everything I want, I'm happy with the joy I've created, and know I can make more.*

have made cherished friends through various social networks like Toastmasters, tennis, volleyball and dance communities—I salsa, ballroom, swing and tango every chance I get—and my eleven year-old son and I have made our own small, happy family in a warm and beautiful little house in Vancouver, on an inlet right next to downtown and a lovely little park with a waterfall, a pond and ducks. If I don't have exactly everything I want, I'm happy with the joy I've created, and know I can make more.

Life presents us with plenty of obstacles. Don't let your spirit be crushed by disappointment and struggle. A resurrection of hope is always within your power—and it's always a great time to set your life on fire!

Linda Christensen, founder and co-host of Conscious Living Radio (www. ConsciousLivingRadio.org), holds a BA, MA, MTS and PhD in religious studies and teaches college and university-level courses in Western, Eastern and new religions. Trained at Hollyhock Institute with Judith Gass as a transformational coach and as a certified hypnotist with

Set Your Life on Fire

Success Coach Technologies, she is a motivational speaker and conducts seminars and on-line courses. Linda conducts a local "Philosopher's Café" on spiritual topics, and has led "Soulful Living" circles and alternative spiritual services, drawing from all traditions, that she calls "Phoenix Rising."

Linda is the executive producer and host of the Fire Up Your Soul *radio show with the Media On Tap network and has been featured on* CBC Newsworld, *Global TV and the* Bill Good Show. *Read her blog and learn about her workshops, online courses, group seminars and setting your own life on fire at www.DrLindaChristensen.com.*

Position Yourself for Greatness

Brendon Burchard

Before I share my story with you, I'm going to put you on the spot and ask you a tough question: What are you worth? Or if it's easier for you to think in terms of exchanging time for money, what is your *time* worth?

What if I told you that no matter what dollar amount you just came up with, you could earn ten, twenty, one hundred times that amount simply by positioning yourself intelligently? What if you could get paid five hundred thousand dollars in one weekend? How would that change your life?

You may think that sounds impossible, but that's exactly what I did. The first seminar I ever did brought in five hundred thousand dollars in one weekend. I'm not sharing this number with you to boast; I'm offering you a glimpse of what is possible for you. Yes, *you*.

Right now you might be thinking that you and I are fundamentally different, that I have the "golden touch" or some mysterious, innate ability that you could never cultivate. Not true. The reality is, you are probably better off than I was when I first started out. I guarantee you have more expertise in your industry than I had in mine at the time. I was twenty-five years old when I started my business, so it's also likely that you have more accumulated knowledge and life experience than I had.

The key to my success is: I positioned myself to play at an elite level right out of the gate. It wasn't as if I coasted into that landmark half-million dollar weekend. I was struggling, but I was also hard at work establishing my place as an expert— as *the* expert—in my field. No matter who you are, or where

---

The key to my success is: I positioned myself to play at an elite level right out of the gate.

---

you come from, or how big your aspirations are, positioning yourself as an expert is the most lucrative thing you will ever do. I believe that wholeheartedly, because it is true for me and for the countless other dreamers and doers I have trained to succeed as experts.

While half a million in one weekend may be hard to wrap your head around, what if you could earn one tenth of that? That's still a game-changing, life-altering amount! I'm guessing you're worth more than you're earning right now, especially if you're being paid by the hour. And I'm sure it's safe to say that whatever amount you think you *could* earn is still a fraction of what you *will* earn when you are perceived as the go-to expert in your field.

No matter what job, industry or entrepreneurial endeavor you are involved in, your income and your influence in life right now is directly proportionate to the number of people who consider you to be an expert. In a relatively short time, I built the largest leadership program, the largest innovation program and the largest partnership program in history, and I accomplished all of this because I cracked the "expert" code. I discovered what all of the great speakers, trainers and coaches have in common, eight strategies that, when followed, will take you to elite expert status and dramatically increase your worth.

The very first strategy, and chief among them, is choosing mastery. Real experts choose to focus on mastering one area, rather than divert their attention to several areas. Most entrepreneurs get impatient or distracted by other opportunities and stop short of mastery, bouncing around from one idea to the next.

Let me give you a metaphor to help you understand what I'm talking about. Imagine you are prospecting for gold. On one side of you is a prospector who is sure he's going to hit gold. He's stoked! He digs enthusiastically for about an hour and finds a few specks of gold, just a little dust really, and then suddenly sets his tools down and walks away in search of a different spot to dig, or better tools. Pretty soon he's got holes everywhere, but no gold.

On the other side of you is a different caliber of prospector. She too found a little gold dust right away, but instead of abandoning her location in search of something better, she chose to keep digging. She is faster, stronger and smarter than the other prospectors, singularly focused on her hole. She digs and digs and digs and does not give up until she hits gold. True experts master something very specific—they dig until they hit gold.

True experts master something very specific—they dig until they hit gold.

Mastery requires study, the second strategy. True experts study their subject. They read everything they can—articles, online content and books, sometimes four books a month on their area of expertise. They attend seminars and classes in their field. They interview mentors and other experts, looking for patterns and best practices. That's how Tony Robbins built his whole career, looking for patterns. The entire multi-hundred billion-dollar consulting industry is built on choosing mastery and recommending best practices.

Third, experts create arguments around what to pay attention to, what things mean, how things work and how things might turn out. The next time you watch the news, pay attention to the experts. Notice that they all say exactly the same things. An expert on the oil industry might first direct your attention to escalating prices, then explain what's behind the increase, then go into a an explanation of why this happened and finally predict what effect rising oil prices will have on the average consumer, or the economy in general—you get the picture. If you're not pointing out all four arguments, you're not positioning yourself effectively as an expert, which means you are limiting your worth.

The fourth strategy experts utilize is simplifying complex ideas by building frameworks. A great example of this is Stephen Covey's *The Seven Habits of Highly Effective People.* Covey broke his ideas down into seven core habits, making them easy for everyone to understand, which is why his book is still a best-seller more than twenty years later.

The next strategy will not only help position you as an expert, it will generate massive amounts of revenue. All great experts write, speak, record and package their knowledge in some way. Maybe they write a book, or a blog or a newsletter. Maybe they speak at conferences, in boardrooms or at events. Whenever they meet with their team, or speak in front of an audience, they make recordings and package their ideas into products—on paper, on the web, on video or audio—and sell them.

Great experts aren't just people with ideas, they are people with a solid business foundation from which they campaign and promote their expertise. This strategy can really take you to the next level, because if you don't promote yourself consistently and *persistently,* you will never earn what you're worth.

The seventh strategy real experts follow is, they charge more than you ever thought they would. If you've ever hired a lawyer or an accountant, you know what I'm talking about! In the speaking and coaching world, the earnings are even more than you could imagine. This is because these people have honed their expertise and *they decided to charge that much.* They didn't let the industry determine their worth; they *declared* their worth and set their own fees. Real experts charge expert fees.

I'll never forget the first time I charged a thousand dollars per month to coach somebody. I could not believe anyone would pay *me* so much to coach them, yet I had been adding value and increasing my expertise. I was worth it, and because I continued to position myself intelligently, I was able to keep increasing my rates. You probably should be charging more for your expertise *now*. Don't wait until you've read fifty books on your industry and created your own live event. Increase your rates today. Even if you're working for somebody else, go after that raise. You are worth it.

The final strategy that real experts use is building a business that is focused on three things: distinction, excellence and service. Experts want to stand out from the crowd, to add

---

Real experts charge expert fees.

---

value in a different way. They want to be the best in their field, exemplifying high standards. Above all, they want to provide fantastic customer service and *be of service*—to give back to their community, to their industry, to the world. I've seen this pattern in the "greats" over and over again.

These eight strategies are the key to positioning yourself as an elite expert, one who commands top dollar for your time, your voice, your ideas and your products. If I knew then what I know now, our business would be quadruple what it is today. At age thirty, I started applying the positioning techniques I just shared with you and built a phenomenal business in less than two years. The reality is, you can do it too. It's not just about making more money; it's about positioning yourself to succeed in all areas, to make the MOST of your idea, your experience, your passion, your *life*.

If you employed the eight strategies I credit to my success, what *could* you be worth tomorrow, next month, next year? Let me assure you again that your value is higher than you could possibly imagine.

So let me ask you again—what are you worth?

Brendon Burchard is the author of Life's Golden Ticket *and* The Student Leadership Guide, *and a highly acclaimed leadership speaker, seminar leader and business consultant. Brendon was blessed to receive life's golden ticket—a second chance—after surviving a dramatic car accident in a developing country. Since then, he has dedicated his life to helping individuals, teams and organizations create and master change. Brendon's books, newsletters, products and appearances now inspire nearly two million people each month.*

As one of the top leadership and motivational speakers in the world, Brendon's authentic, powerful and hilarious presentations have become legendary. His past clients include eBay, Best Buy, Levi's and thousands of executives and entrepreneurs. He has shared the stage with the greats—Tony Robbins, Deepak Chopra and others—and with the Dalai Lama and Sir Richard Branson, inspiring others to be more giving and compassionate while building their businesses. Brendon created the Partnership Seminar, the first to teach social entrepreneurs and experts how to partner with nonprofit organizations and Fortune 500 companies to grow their business and change the world. He is also the founder of the Experts Academy, the first comprehensive training seminar to reveal the secrets of how "gurus" build their expert empires as authors, coaches and speakers.

Brendon's message—that each of us is called to live by conscious choice and to contribute to others—has changed thousands of lives around the globe. He is the founder of The Global Partnership Summit, an innovative program that brings together Fortune 500 CEOs, global nonprofit leaders and five hundred social entrepreneurs to create partnerships that address the world's most pressing issues. Brendon brokered the largest global nonprofit partnership in history, which now teaches nine million youth about leadership, business and service. Brendon donates a portion of the proceeds from the sale of his works to Junior Achievement and Kiwanis International. He lives in Portland, Oregon, with his incredible wife, Denise. To learn more about Brendon, visit www.BrendonBurchard.com.

A Circle Called Love

Sajeela Cormack

D o you want to be a warning to others, an example of a life lived sleepwalking and suffering—or do you want to be an inspiring role model for what *can* be?

Are you open to the possibility of changing, growing, coming out of a sleepy state of blaming other people and living in victimhood and fear?

Are you open to living the possibility of a greater purpose, a purpose shaped by giving back and making a difference just by being who you are?

My greatest accomplishment is my transformation from warning to inspiration. Twenty-six years ago I had no self-worth. This was the result of how I had interpreted my upbringing; from that dark place I had lived the way I thought others wanted me to. As a product of other people's thinking, I had accepted a life of blame, reaction, martyrdom, conditional love and self-persecution. I was filled with self-loathing, pain and turmoil—I was tossed powerlessly between high and low extremes of emotion.

Suffering from crippling arthritis and daily massive migraines, I lived with tremendous physical pain. A chiropractic adjustment left me bedridden, and my husband, feeling sure that he could not take care of me, sent me to my mother who lived many miles away. The doctors said I was in the middle of a nervous breakdown; they prescribed antidepressants that took me further down.

One day I reached for a bottle to take an overdose and try to end my life. With no sense of self, no solid foundation, I felt I was not even worthy enough to raise my own children; I was sure this was the best thing I could do—and that I had no other choice.

But I did have a choice; the suicide attempt was a major turning point. I recovered and began to heal, thanks to the love and nurturing from my mother and friends who continued to believe in me. The *conscious* turning point came when I began to meditate; that's when I woke up and started living from a new paradigm.

A friend told me that with his help, I could quit the antidepressants within a week. I thought he was full of himself; I'd been told I'd be on the drugs for the rest of my life. "I'll give you three weeks, then," he said. "I dare you

---

Are you open to living the possibility of a greater purpose, a purpose shaped by giving back and making a difference just by being who you are?

---

to prove me wrong." He asked for a commitment of ninety days: if I missed one day, then I'd go back to day one and start all over again. The first day I meditated, though, I didn't have a migraine. On the second day, the same result. After seven days of meditating without migraines, my life was changed.

Two weeks after my friend had issued his challenge—his invitation—I was off all the medications and was so proud of myself!

Then I began to read. My friend fed my mind with books—teachings from Osho, Buddha, Krishna, Jesus, Zen, Taoism—I began to get a new perspective on life, and I began to let go of the past. I began to swim—and I did yoga and Tai Chi every day. I immersed myself in nature to receive its teachings.

Thanks to active meditation, reading and my eagerness to improve my life, I was led to a variety of personal development studies that taught me to implement new ideas and ask better questions. Better questions gave me better answers. My

---

Active meditation was the key. When I began to meditate, instead of merely reacting, a gap developed between a circumstance happening and the effect it had on me. In that gap, I saw that I had a choice.

---

teachers became my family, supporting me until I was strong enough to stand up and say, "This is who I am now," to those who didn't understand the changes I'd experienced. Then, because I was now practicing being my own best friend, I was able to communicate consciously and from the heart, inspiring others in my life to change—and heal. Active meditation was the key. When I began to meditate, instead of merely reacting, a gap developed between a circumstance happening and the effect it had on me. In that gap, I saw that I had a choice.

I could think for a moment, and then come up with a way to respond that would serve me better. Through meditation I became calm and more centered. I felt more playful—and kind, caring and understanding with my children. I was filled with energy, hope and possibility. Because of that, I've been meditating for twenty-six years—and the more busy I am, the more committed I am to meditation, because I know what it does for me. I no longer live in the darkness of fear and hurt; I live a conscious life in the light of joy and love and possibility.

I learned that our thoughts determine what we project out into our lives—it is our own minds that create or remove obstacles. A problem, challenge or illness cannot be overcome at the same level of consciousness in which we created it. When we're anxious enough for our circumstances to change, we do things differently—and we get different results! No different action equals the same result. Different or new results excite us, feed our optimism and open our minds to new possibilities. All these results help us to transcend the obstacles we created in the first place.

Perhaps the simplest way to explain this is by sharing my three most important mottos:

> *If it's to be, it's up to me.*
> *Seek first to understand, then to be understood.*
> *There's no failure, only feedback.*

It's one thing to repeat these statements, but to live them is an entirely different experience. Now, when somebody makes me wrong I no longer think, "I'm a terrible person, I'm a failure." Instead, I say to myself, "This is feedback, it's not failure. How

---

Let me see what I can do—now, not later. As a rule, people do not live in the moment—they concentrate on escaping the pain of the past, or they focus on some future excitement that distracts them from the discomfort or pleasure of where they are right now.

---

do I wish to interpret this feedback? How do I wish to feel? Let me first seek to understand them and their perspective, and then invite this person to be open to understanding me and my viewpoint." Then I go back to the primary motto: If it's to be, it's up to me.

Let me see what I can do—now, not later. As a rule, people do not live in the moment—they concentrate on escaping the pain of the past, or they focus on some future excitement that distracts them from the discomfort or pleasure of where they are right now. I find consistently that right now, this very moment, is always just gorgeous—in fact, it's perfect! If I put a judgment on it that says it's *not* gorgeous, that's gorgeous too, because it's telling me something.

Picture a triangle. One corner is "persecution," another "victim," and the last "rescuer." In the middle of the triangle is "FEAR." Instead of living a triangular life—in which we persecute and make victims of ourselves, and then project

---

Don't let old conditioning keep you from becoming and enjoying everything you are capable of. You can be an inspiration to all around you—and even to yourself.

---

that outward onto others who persecute, victimize and (maybe) rescue us—we can *transcend* this whole paradigm by replacing it with an entirely new paradigm, one in which we live in love, *be* love, tell the whole truth—and take complete responsibility for the creation of the whole of our own realities.

Living a personally conscious, optimistic, evolved life means being an inspiring role model of open, heart-filled, conscious communication in which you are the choice-maker and the responder. Your attitude of thankful optimism colors your whole experience as you journey to your desired destination, and you tend not to create any more resistance to the flowering of your own success—or not any more than what you can handle. You're not controlled by your reactions; instead you take what rings true for you and leave the rest.

In my former life, I'd wake each day to sadness, guilt and anxiety, struggling through the pain-laden day until I fell asleep crying. Now, my days begin and end with love, gratitude, prayer and meditation. In joy now I skip along the beach! People can't help but smile when they see me.

You too have a choice. If you have the courage to do something differently—even once—you'll get different results. There is nothing that practice does not improve. Don't let old conditioning keep you from becoming and enjoying everything you are capable of. You can be an inspiration to all around you—and even to yourself.

I invite you to open your heart—and join the circle of love that is your birthright. Your value is already established by virtue of your sacred creation.

Sajeela Cormack is a thought leader who specializes in cooperative entrepreneurship and personal sustainability. She is the co-author of the best-selling book The Law of Business Attraction *and three other books. She is CEO of Life Architects™ Pty Ltd, a company dedicated to the awakening of human consciousness, cooperative capitalism and the raising of the world's living standards.*

Based in Australia, Sajeela travels the world facilitating, consulting, coaching and speaking at events that truly change lives. Her impact is strengthened by her experience in positive psychology, NLP, meditation, holistic alkalizing health and the Open-up Communication System. Sajeela also shares her inspirational messages, which are focused on empowering people who are interested in their own personal growth to create balance; to build a cooperative business model that forms a playground for transformation and to achieve a level of all-around wellness and business success that is positive and sustainable. www. SajeelaCormack.com

Just Say I'm Sorry

Judy Wilson

How do you heal a broken heart? How do you rebuild bridges long broken, amend the wrongs you can't forget and restore relationships with the people you miss most of all? Is it even *possible* to expect forgiveness, reunion or a fresh start? Yes. Yes, it most definitely is! All of this is possible when you make an earnest effort to make amends.

When I was sixteen years old, I broke two hearts. In the fall of 1969, I sent a "Dear John" letter to my boyfriend Tom—and spent the next thirty-two years wishing I could take it back. I met Tom Procter at a church dance when I was fourteen years old. We dated on and off, and eventually got pretty serious. I loved everything about Tom, but it was his excitement about life and the future that really got me hooked.

Growing up in Southern California was loads of fun because there was so much to do. My brother Tim was one of Tom's good friends, and the three of us, along with Tim's date, would drive around Los Angeles in Tom's bright orange '54 Chevy. Sometimes we went to tapings of *The Newlywed Game* and *The Dating Game*. Just before I turned sixteen, I broke my leg skiing. Tom took me to the prom anyway, full hip cast and all.

Two months later, just after Tom graduated from high school, his parents moved their family to a small farm in Southern Utah.

His father had decided to go into a business partnership raising rabbits that would later be used for a new skin grafting process on Vietnam veterans who had been burned by napalm. Tom and I weren't happy about the move, but since I had two years left of school, we had no choice but to stick it out and love each other from a distance. On one trip before the actual move, I drove with Tom and his family to see his new home in Utah. During the long drive he said, "I want you to marry me when you're finished with school."

It wasn't the most romantic proposal; now that I think of it, it wasn't really a proposal at all, more a statement of fact. But my heart leapt just as if he had gotten down on one knee and handed me the Hope Diamond! It was decided. As soon as I graduated, I would move to Utah and become a rabbit farmer, too.

When I was sixteen years old, I broke two hearts. In the fall of 1969, I sent a "Dear John" letter to my boyfriend Tom—and spent the next thirty-two years wishing I could take it back.

We couldn't wait, though; we were young and in love, and two years seemed like an eternity. So we hatched a plan to get Tom back to California. Shortly after the move, Tim and I went to visit Tom and his family. The Chevy broke down on the way to pick us up from the Greyhound Bus Terminal, and we ended up walking through Spanish Fork Canyon in the middle of the night. I still remember that walk; after six months, my hip cast had finally just come off, and though the walk was long and the canyon dark, seeing Tom again made that night a magical experience.

After we arrived at the farm, we packed some of Tom's clothes and hid them in the trunk of his car. One night, we told his dad we were going to a drive-in movie—but drove back to California instead. I suppose it wouldn't have been too difficult to find us in Tom's car: earlier in the year, he had used one of his mom's tablecloths as a stencil and spray-painted a brown lace "mist" pattern on the top of the orange Chevy!

Our parents discussed the situation while we were on the road, and when we finally arrived in California, it was mutually decided that Tom could stay at our house for the rest of the summer. It was an amazing summer, full of fun and promises. As

---

I knew, the moment after I placed the letter in the mailbox, that I had done the wrong thing.

---

it came to a close, Tom returned to Utah to help with the farm and get ready for college. The day he left was one of the most painful days of my life. During our tearful wait for his flight at the airport, we heard Peter, Paul and Mary's song, "Leaving on a Jet Plane." It became "our song."

That fall we talked on the phone, and wrote letters I saved as treasures. But as time passed, it was harder to stay close when there was so much distance between us. In early October, Tom called to tell me his father had passed away from a heart attack. Later in the week, he called again to ask me to drive up to Utah with his sister to be with him for the funeral, but I never received the message. Back then I was young, just about to enter my junior year in high school, and had no idea how to handle a long-term, long-distance relationship. So, in an impetuous move, I wrote Tom a letter breaking off our relationship. I knew, the moment after I placed the letter in the mailbox, that I had done the wrong thing.

I didn't hear from Tom after that, and by the time I went back to look for him, his family had been forced to move from the farm after the death of his father. I had no idea how to find him. In my heart of hearts, I knew that I had made a huge mistake, and I missed Tom terribly. But what could I do? It was 1969, decades before the Internet made it easy to find people.

So I did what most people do when they can't go back—I went forward. I married, had children, got an education and built a career. Tom was always in my heart, though, and in the back of my mind.

The realization that I had hurt him deeply and unnecessarily haunted me, so I started my quest to find him. For years, whenever I visited Utah, I looked for him, his mom or his sisters in the phone book, and when I traveled, I looked up his name in local phone books. Later, when I had access to the Internet, I looked for Tom and his family in company directories and on other websites. I began the recovery process for alcohol addiction in 1981, and it was then that I discovered the power of making amends. I realized that my heart would never heal until I had a chance to apologize to Tom.

In 2001, I served on the committee for my thirty-year high school reunion. Looking for alumni, I contacted Shelly, one of my old friends. She pulled out her yearbook to find my picture and noticed the note I wrote to her: "Tom Procter and Judy Nielsen— forever and always." When she asked if we were still together, I knew I still loved him. And I knew I had to give it one more try—not because I wanted a relationship with him again, but just to be able to tell him how sorry I was for ending our relationship the way I did.

One day, out of nowhere, two of Tom's sisters showed up in my search. I was so excited to finally find them, and filled with the hope that I might see Tom again. I emailed back and forth with his sisters, and after a few days, Tom called me! It was as if no time had passed at all; his voice sounded exactly the same. How is this for a coincidence: he had just moved back to California four months earlier, and we were living less than one hundred miles from each other! We made arrangements to meet the following week.

I offered Tom my sincere apology for the way I had ended things, for ending things at all. He accepted my apology right away. It was such a huge relief! I apologized to many people in my recovery process, but making amends to Tom was the scariest of all. It is one of the greatest personal accomplishments of my life. I have such peace, joy and serenity in my life now that I have fully made amends with Tom.

No matter what you've done, how deep the hurt or how many years have gone by, you can heal your heart. It begins with a simple, yet powerful step: just say you're sorry. Making amends is a process of letting go of regret, and releasing all of the negative feelings associated with whatever you believe you did wrong.

> *No matter what you've done, how deep the hurt or how many years have gone by, you can heal your heart. It begins with a simple, yet powerful step: just say you're sorry.*

A simple, heartfelt apology can break down walls and repair old bonds. I've seen it in my workshops: people light up inside; they're lighter, happier and more confident. Even if the person you've hurt isn't ready to accept your apology or begin again, just saying you're sorry will restore peace to your mind and your heart.

You might be wondering what happened after our long-awaited meeting in the restaurant. This story, like so many stories of making amends and acceptance, has a happy ending. When Tom got out of his car that day we met again, I thought, "Oh my God, he's gorgeous!" All of the old feelings came rushing back, and I knew without a doubt that I still loved him. We had both changed physically, but I still saw a young man. Tom and I have been together, happily, for the past eight years. We found our way back to our young love, the love that never died. I feel like a teenager around him, and my heart, at last, has healed.

Everyone lives with regrets, to some extent. We have all done things we're not proud of, things we wish we could go back in time and handle differently. One mistake can haunt you forever. It can eat away at you, take away your peace of mind and call sadness to you, while preventing you from taking chances in love and life.

Just do it!

Just say: "I'm sorry," and watch with wonder at the power of making amends. You *can* heal a broken heart. You do it one apology at a time.

Judy Wilson is on a mission to help people break free from the prison of regret and guilt and move on with their lives. Judy's recovery journey began on July 14, 1981, the day she took her last drink of alcohol. As she worked the steps, Judy came to understand the tremendous healing power of making amends, and later went on to facilitate groups in the process of making amends. A graduate of the University of San Francisco with a degree in organizational behavior, she works with Lisa Nichol's acclaimed program "Motivating the Teen Spirit," helping young people fall in love with themselves again and make integrity-based decisions. To learn more about Judy and how to make amends, and to share your own apology story with others, visit www.JustSayImSorry.com.

Never Give Up On Giving Back

Jim Lorigo

Y ou know that certain kind of individual who always looks on the bright side and never gives up? The guy who isn't afraid to take risks because he knows the only failure is in not trying at all?

Well, I'm blessed to be that guy, the guy who always finds a way, no matter what the challenges or obstacles may be.

Success comes to those who are not only motivated to create opportunities, but who also accept the risks that come with implementing new and creative ideas. Successful people do not self-sabotage, nor do we allow others to sabotage our dreams. And a "can do" attitude, backed up with creative problem-solving, can move mountains.

These are the principles on which I built my financial services business, and it is this philosophy that helped me reach the top one percent of earners in my industry. Despite my accomplishments, though, I once had a persistent, unsettled feeling that there was more to life. I knew there was a level of fulfillment beyond money and material things, beyond accolades. I knew there was something else out there for me that would truly enrich my life.

Looking back, it's quite clear that what I was feeling was spiritual emptiness. But at the time, I felt a void I could not define. And then, one day, I found my mission.

It struck me about four years ago, at a charity event my wife, Toni, and I attended near our home in Denver. We had participated in many charitable causes over the years, but this event was quite different. We watched a brief film about children orphaned due to preventable illnesses, and children living with disabilities who would never have the chance to lead normal lives. The heartache they experienced was palpable.

Something in the film dug deep into my heart and soul. I knew, instantly, that from that day forward I would commit myself to charitable giving. I was determined to give back, and

> I knew there was a level of fulfillment beyond money and material things, beyond accolades. I knew there was something else out there for me that would truly enrich my life.

to do so in a big way. It was my turn, plain and simple. I knew that the event's staff and volunteers would be rewarded for their labors, adding new donations from that night's event to their already successful fundraising. But I also knew there had to be a smarter—or perhaps easier—way to raise money.

I didn't know it at the time, but I was about to embark on a journey which would transform the world of charitable giving— as well as my own life. In dedicating my time and talents to find a way for charities, churches and foundations to raise significant funds with much less, if not minimal, effort, I felt a renewed sense of purpose—one based in helping others rather than helping myself achieve and accumulate more.

With a new sense of determination, I worked tirelessly over the next several months to design a plan that was both financially sound *and* innovative. My wife and my entire staff, sharing my enthusiasm, cheered me on.

Over the course of my forty years in business, I had cultivated many close relationships with colleagues in the financial services and insurance industries. These bonds helped me go right where I wanted to go to propose my new idea: the top.

I explained to countless CEOs, boards of directors and key managers how they could be part of this dynamic new concept, helping to raise millions for charitable purposes. I traveled back and forth across the country heralding my message. I felt utterly confident in my idea; in-depth and persistent research proved that it could be done. My energy and excitement grew daily.

After one year, however, I was still unable to secure the funding required to get the project off the ground. I was frustrated. After all, I had been able to overcome obstacles in the past. Why was this project different? I had traveled for one full year, spent time away from my business and invested a considerable amount of money in the creation of presentations,

---

I would never abandon my dream of reshaping and enhancing the concept of charitable giving. I simply would not give up.

---

websites and brochures. More importantly, I had given up quality time with my family. And yet, despite all of this, I could not make it happen. I was stunned. As the guy who had always overcome every obstacle, this inability to bring my concept to fruition was inconceivable.

Was I ready to say, "Enough is enough!" and shelve the project? What would happen, then, to that never-give-up, motivated guy? What actually went wrong? Could I have done something differently? What vital piece was I missing?

"How can I possibly quit?" I asked my wife.

But at this point, I had no choice, no matter what the answers were. I had to admit that it was time to move forward with "Plan B." I had to roll up my sleeves and shift my focus back to my financial business. As heartbroken as I was, I knew that I had given it my all. What amazes me is that, no matter how deflated and defeated I felt, I still knew the flame of hope for my charitable project could never be extinguished. I would never abandon my dream of reshaping and enhancing the concept of charitable giving. I simply would not give up.

Sometimes an answer comes when you least expect it. While attending a financial seminar last year, my mind wandered— straight into the most incredible "aha" moment. In an instant, I saw the solution. It was clear. I had discovered the missing piece of the puzzle that had eluded me for four years!

"Thank you God!" I prayed. "I always knew you'd share the answer with me."

Now, because I held fast to my dream even when it seemed impossible, The Gift of Love is poised to raise one billion dollars over the next ten years.

The realization that my epiphany was a gift from God inspired the name of my charitable giving concept. What better label to give my project than "The Gift of Love?"

After all the disappointment I had experienced, I understood, finally, that it had only served to make my "aha" moment even more rewarding. I had been given that critical piece, the keystone that would transform my charitable giving concept into reality. I went back to the drawing board directly, this time knowing that I was right on track. I was finally able to see that with just this one slight twist on the original concept, there would be no barriers to getting funding. With this new insight, I would finally be able to bring my plan to bear, providing the means for charitable organizations to further their causes by raising millions more dollars each year.

I've often heard that "out of bad comes good." Having reviewed my initial approach to the project with a much more critical eye, I incorporated a team approach that used the expertise of the many tax attorneys, CPAs, security licensed and financial planning associates that I had built strong relationships with over the years. Today, together, we do more—and do better—for charitable organizations everywhere.

Four years ago I fell in love with the dream of making a *real* difference in the world by "expanding the good" that charitable organizations strive to create. Now, because I held fast to my dream even when it seemed impossible, The Gift of Love is poised to raise one billion dollars over the next ten years.

Tough times don't last, but tough people do. Despite our best efforts, we all face challenges in our lives. But there is no shame in that. If you get knocked down, get back up. If you are heartbroken about a failure to accomplish something you are truly passionate about, leave a corner of your heart open to the possibility—the *probability*—that your dream can come true. Just let your passion sustain you through the tough times. The rewards will be unimaginable!

James C. Lorigo is founder and President of Americorp Services, Inc. In his forty years as a licensed insurance professional, Jim has helped hundreds of clients nationwide simplify and secure their retirements by using a variety of tax-efficient strategies to maximize growth while minimizing taxation.

Jim takes an educational approach when helping his clients retire with financial security and peace of mind. He also works with charities, churches and non-profits to increase philanthropic contributions from their donor members while significantly augmenting the financial legacies of these donor members.

Jim is married, has two children and is the proud grandfather of three. He and his wife, Toni, are long-time Denver residents and are passionately committed to a variety of volunteer activities and philanthropic interests.

An Outlaw's Odyssey

Paul E. Hendricks

For most of my life, I was an outlaw and a misfit, a selfish and destructive child of a man. I hurt people. I broke things. I wrecked the days I lived in. Then I changed. Gradually, painfully and oftentimes reluctantly, I changed. My life is now a mission to share the principles of forgiveness, compassion and unconditional love with the rest of humanity; to teach Universal laws and help others live extraordinary lives. Sure, it seems farfetched—but I'm living an extraordinary life, and a few years ago nothing could have seemed more farfetched than that.

I grew up in Cleveland and went to a private, Christian prep school. My household was full of religion, and it was also full of violence. Back then, I couldn't reconcile that dichotomy. Now I can. I know that, as violent as my childhood home was, it was the Boy Scouts compared to the homes my parents grew up in. It wasn't *the* best, but it was *their* best, and I can forgive them—now. Back then, my response was to turn to violence and drugs. I was overflowing with anger. The Law of Attraction works both ways. I attracted anger because I was angry. I was a magnet for destructive behavior because I was a walking tower of destruction.

This cycle of violence, drugs and self-sabotage followed me everywhere I went, for years: Europe, Oklahoma, New York, Virginia. But it all started to change the day my girlfriend, Diane, left me. We were living in Washington, D.C., and she just couldn't watch me self-destruct anymore. She moved five thousand miles away to Hawaii and I cast myself down a hole. I had a drug dealer move in with me. One night, I decided to kill myself. I took all of his cocaine, dumped it on a plate, grabbed a bottle of Jack Daniels and started laying into all of it.

Then, I felt something wet on my neck. I thought it was the ceiling leaking. I looked up. It was Titan, a pit bull I'd rescued in Maryland. I'd rescued him because I didn't think anyone else would. He was licking me and looking at me with eyes that said,

> *I was a magnet for destructive behavior because I was a walking tower of destruction.*

"Who's going to take care of me?" I realized I was responsible for another living being, and that snapped me out of my own little bubble of depression. I realized it didn't have to be this way. It is nearly impossible to be depressed if you're concerned with the welfare of someone—or something—else.

The next morning I went out for coffee with Titan. Sitting outside, I looked at my dog and said, "Well, today's a day I didn't expect to have. What do I do now?" Once again, his eyes spoke to me: "Go get Mommy," they said. So I moved to Hawaii, and we started over completely. Diane didn't think it was going to work. I did.

I got a job as a loan officer. One day, I had a tantrum in front of everyone in the office, and my supervisor said, "Paul, you are a beacon of negativity." Later that night, he gave me a copy of the book, *The Way of the Peaceful Warrior.* I went home and inhaled it. And then I read it again. I realized that I was going through life as a reactor. That's how I'd always been. If I wanted to have a happy, joyous life, I needed to become proactive. I needed to own my feelings.

I immersed myself in the process of change. I read everything I could. I went to transformational seminars. I got into martial arts and started meditating. I started writing a book about my journey. I wrote in first person so that the reader could experience what I was experiencing. But writing about me was a risk and fear crept in. And I responded to fear as I always had: with booze and drugs.

That didn't work. I was writing a book about abusing myself and I was still using drugs. Not all of the time. Drugs went from being the rule to being the exception. Still, I was doing them, so I shelved the book and got a job as a case manager. As soon as I got the job, I went out to party with a friend and woke up the next morning on a patio, covered in vomit. I went to my new job and was surprised with a drug test. I failed it.

I was going to fight the firing—until I had a moment of clarity and grace. I realized that I had created this mess called my life. I thought I was a superhero who could find drugs whenever I wanted. It was my "Negative" Law of Attraction in full throttle. Even though I hadn't gone out with the intention of finding drugs, I'd found them, blacked out, puked on myself and lost my

---

If I wanted to have a happy, joyous life, I needed to become proactive. I needed to own my feelings.

---

new job. I went for a walk on the beach, looked up to the sky and realized that I was creating my own cycle of self-sabotage. That was my moment of surrender.

Three weeks later, I went to a seminar. It was a weekend of me looking at myself in a mirror—and it was the first time I owned my life; every experience, effective and ineffective. All of us, as we're raised, start limiting our beliefs and potential by judging our experiences. I had been told over and over that I was a piece of crap and I believed it. Someone finally said, "So what? Now what? You're not living in that world anymore, but you keep making it happen." I had perpetuated the story that I was unworthy of love, success and happiness, and it was time to make something new happen. I left that seminar realizing that I was the architect of my own life.

The seminar reconnected me with my God. I realized that all along I had been denying my own spirituality, the God in me. Given the amount of drugs I'd taken, I should have died; but for some reason, I hadn't. I believed I was still alive because God wanted to use me as a messenger, through writing and speaking.

A big part of my message is that we have this illusion that we're separate and we find ways to make that true. But we're not separate. The message was in my story, which showed the power of the human spirit. I wanted to show people that we are our own biggest obstacles and that we can do what we want to do when we're in alignment. But I had to prove that by writing the book. So I wrote the book.

I also started speaking publicly about my story. Amazingly, people listened. And they gave me feedback, saying that my story inspired them, saying I was effective because I didn't tell them that my life was perfect. My story showed them that life isn't bad. In fact, it is a gift. Through my story, I was telling them that their lives were all about their perceptions. As Wayne Dyer says, "When you change the way you look at things, the things you look at change."

People need to look at themselves with a different set of glasses to find out what's prohibiting them from living extraordinary lives. I help people see that. I help them find those limiting beliefs and start recognizing them for what they are: illusions. During the first half of my speaking engagements I share my story. Then I flip to audience interaction, using visualizations and affirmations to have them focus on what they want and to give them the tools to get there.

So many people get locked up in a narrow interpretation of the American Dream. They back themselves into a tiny box and find themselves swimming in debt, unhappy and living without a purpose. Even though they've done everything they were "supposed" to do, they're still not happy because they're not living the extraordinary lives they were put on this earth to live. They have to get out of that box, get uncomfortable, take risks and pursue their dreams. Everybody has a golden touch in life, something they're extraordinary at. If they're not utilizing that golden touch, they're not being true to who they are or who they want to be. As a result, they're taking from themselves and they're taking from other people.

When people are doing what they're passionate about, they're in alignment and start attracting what they need. After finishing my book, I spoke with publishers who were interested, but ultimately decided to publish it on my own. At the time, I had one editor and knew nothing about publishing. Within a

Recognizing limiting beliefs and being able to switch my thoughts are the most valuable tools I have to offer and to use. They change my attitude from, "Can't," to, "You better believe I can."

few months I had a team of editors, proofreaders, web designers, graphic designers and branding people. I'm constantly attracting people who support my platform. Simply operating from love rather than fear has made all the difference in what I create and attract.

I'm still my biggest obstacle, although I'm learning how to get out of my own way a lot more. I give myself to life a lot more fully. When my book comes out, I know I'll look like an ass in much of it; but that's because I acted like an ass. I no longer cower from the truth about me. I experience feelings, I don't numb myself out and I've learned the importance of forgiveness and not judging other people. I found that every solution to every obstacle is available to me through meditation and prayer. Recognizing limiting beliefs and being able to switch my thoughts are the most valuable tools I have to offer and to use. They change my attitude from, "Can't," to, "You better believe I can."

When I wake up in the morning, I am grateful that I have another day to create my extraordinary life. I interact with people, and they're a reflection of me and of who I am. I am honored that my passion for writing and speaking has an impact on people that helps turn their lives around. I found my purpose.

Paul E. Hendricks is a breakthrough expert and transformational speaker who believes that every person on this planet has a golden touch, and he helps audiences and individuals learn how to get out of their own way. Paul uses his own story to inspire audiences while sharing tools they can take home to uncover their limiting beliefs and start living their dreams NOW! He accomplishes this by weaving together spoken word, humor, acting, inspirational stories, visualizations and live music.

His own story is available in his book, Wake Up! The Enlightenment of an American Misfit and Outlaw. *To learn more about Paul, his book and his speaking engagements, go to www.PaulEHendricks.com.*

ACT *AS IF!*

Barbara Niven

My dream began when I was a very little girl. I always knew that I was going to be an actress, and I've always loved a camera. In fact, I remember practicing my movie star pose when I was about four years old. My family tells me that when we went on outings, I would disappear—and they would find me down the beach posing and waving in front of some stranger's camera. There must have been a lot of people who said, "Who's the chubby little blonde girl?" when they got their photos back.

Still, I put my dream on hold as I grew up and began to live everybody *else's* dream of what my life was supposed to be like. I had no other kind of role model—nobody I knew was in the arts or entertainment industry. So I quit college after less than a year, got a job, got married, had a baby and started a business with my husband. I always thought, "Someday I'll pursue my acting dream."

One day an application for our ten-year high school reunion came in the mail. I couldn't believe ten years had already gone by. The form asked: "Who did you marry?" "How many kids did you have?" and so on.

The final question was, "Have you achieved all you thought you would in your life by now?" It hit me like a ton of bricks—I hadn't even started!

The first thing I did after my wakeup call was consider my options. I hadn't finished college, and by now I was a single mother with a two-year-old daughter. But I thought, "I can write and I'm great in front of the camera. Why don't I become a broadcast journalist?" Everybody told me it couldn't be done, but that always makes my fight kick in.

I found two mentors. One was the news director at KGW, the NBC affiliate in Portland, and the other was a producer at *PM Magazine.* "If I bring you stories," I asked them, "will you mentor me? Because I *am* going to work for you. And don't tell me what's good. I want to know what to do to make my stories better so you'll hire me." They both took me on.

Everybody told me it couldn't be done, but that always makes my fight kick in.

And this is when I first started to ACT *AS IF!* I began to assume the position and act as if the life I wanted was already happening—until it was. I would call someone, lie through my teeth and say, "Hi, I'm an associate producer with KGW. If I come in and pre-interview you, we may do a story on you. But I need to pre-produce you first."

Of course, everyone wanted to be on TV. So after each interview I would race home and write it up into a script, adding video shots I imagined I would use if I had a real camera. The next day I'd knock on doors again and present my stories to my mentors. They were shocked to see me back so soon! But they liked my moxie, and I was good. And persistent. Finally KGW hired me as an intern, and I sold my very first story to network.

Then I heard that ABC Daytime casting was on a nationwide tour, searching for an actress to replace Tina on *One Life to Live.* They were making a stop in Seattle. It didn't matter that I'd never taken an acting class, I just knew I had to go. I went to a bookstore and picked out a monologue from Neil Simon's "Chapter Two." I didn't perform it for anyone—I practiced it silently, over and over, in my head. I loved it. I could really relate to my character, and I poured my heart and soul into it.

When the day of the audition came, a winter ice storm raged outside. It shut down the whole Pacific Northwest, including the airports. I, however, had waited long enough to put my dream

---

*After that audition, I knew exactly what I wanted.
I had plugged in to my passion—I was home.*

---

into action. So I bundled up, hopped in my car and drove from Portland to Seattle for the casting call. Nobody else was on the road, because it was sheer black ice.

When I got there I changed clothes in the car, fixed my makeup and went in. They put my audition on tape, and ten minutes later I was back in my car, heading home, completely transformed by the performing experience I'd just had. Unbelievably, the next week ABC flew me to New York for a screen test!

That's when I knew I was on the right track. It was a confirmation of deep feelings I've had about myself my whole life. I didn't get the part that time, but, ironically, I *was* on the series twenty years later! After that audition, I knew exactly what I wanted. I had plugged in to my passion—I was home.

When I started my acting career, I was a single mom and almost thirty, which is way older than you're supposed to be in this business. People thought I was crazy! But I did it anyway, because the thought of not at least *trying* was worse than failing. And now I've been making a living acting for over twenty-five years.

I eventually packed up a U-Haul, installed my little daughter as copilot and moved to L.A. It was a real struggle, and at times we were so poor. But we have had an extraordinary life, full of love and support for each other's dreams. My daughter now says that the best gift I ever gave her was teaching her that the secret to life is doing what you love—what you'd do for free—and then figuring out how to make a living at it. You may not be rich in money, but you'll wake up every day excited about your life.

It became my passion and my mission to persuade others that if I can live this crazy dream of being an actress, anybody can do anything, no matter who they are or where they come from. Truly.

You can't just wish for your life to change—you have to take action!

Put your dream out there to the world! And after you've stated it out loud, write it down. Once something is written down, the Universe conspires to make it happen. Then start taking actions to make your dream a reality.

Yes, it's scary, and people will try to hold you back. Most people are just settling in their lives and want to keep you down too, because if you make it, your achievements negate their negativity. Don't let them bring you down. Surround yourself with a supportive web of optimists and action-takers, like the Dreamers Network on my website. It's a place for us dreamers to find mentoring and networking in a setting where no dream is crazy or impossible. We've got to stick together!

I developed my ACT *AS IF!* system to help others manifest their dreams based on what has worked in my own life. It uses acting and motivational techniques to help kick-start the Law of Attraction. For instance, when I was just starting out as an actress, a fan sent me a replica of an Oscar with my name on it. It has sat on my desk ever since, where I can see and feel and touch it as I go after my dream. Bringing a dream from the mental realm to the physical is so important.

Most of us miss the real secret of *The Secret.* There's a missing link between *thinking* and *manifesting.* We can put our intention out there and visualize all we want, but our dreams usually stay locked inside our heads as mere thoughts. It's only when we move our dreams *out* of our heads and into our physical lives that things start to change.

You can't just wish for your life to change—you have to take action! You are the writer, the producer, the director and the star of whatever life you're already living. So if it isn't working for you, change it! Decide what you want, and simply start to ACT *AS IF!* Consciously create your new *you* just as an actor does

> Change doesn't happen all at once, even though we may want it to. It is about progress, not perfection, and about celebration along the way.

every time he picks up a script and creates a new character. Begin living as who you want to be, right now. When you assume the position, your belief system kicks in. When *you* believe, so does everyone else. Gradually, you start to transform, and it becomes your reality.

Change doesn't happen all at once, even though we may want it to. It is about progress, not perfection, and about celebration along the way. I have learned that the idea of perfection is a major trap, and it limits our possibilities. Mine has been an incredible journey, with huge ups and downs and life lessons, but all those have only made me stronger. Each time I hit a wall, I was forced to take stock, change and grow to the next level. I call this process "Reinvent, refocus and rejoice!"

My wonderful, wise acting coach, Milton Katselas, used to say, "The one who gets up from the mat the most times wins." I can't tell you how many times I've been down on that mat, wondering how I'm going to get up again. But I always do, with a new fierceness and a resolve to *make it happen.* That attitude has made all the difference in my career and my life.

Remember, every moment you have a choice. You can go toward your dream or away from it. Please don't settle for less than wonderful in your life. And don't give up five minutes before the miracle! I am living proof that you can make it happen!

Barbara Niven is definitely living her dreams! She's one of Hollywood's busiest actresses, and has served on the National Board of Directors for the Screen Actors Guild. Between film assignments, she is in demand as a presentation and performance coach. Barbara created the breakthrough ACT AS IF! system and speaks about her struggle with and victory over an eating disorder, so that others will speak up about their own secrets and get help. She's profiled in a book called Feeding the Fame: Celebrities Tell Their Real-Life Stories of Eating Disorders and Recovery. *Barbara is currently at work on two books. Check out her website at www.BarbaraNiven.com and join her Dreamers Network. Visit www.ShowBusiness101.com for Barbara's coaching tips.*

Living Full Out

Nancy Solari

I heard, "It's possible you will go blind," when the doctor gave me the news. I just didn't believe it would *really* happen. With contacts, I could see just fine. He could be wrong, I reasoned, or maybe it wouldn't be *as bad* as he predicted. I was only sixteen when I was diagnosed with retinitis pigmentosa (RP), a degenerative eye condition with no cure in sight. And I had big dreams. Huge dreams. Going blind was not in the plan. In that moment, it would have been so easy to surrender to the diagnosis—but in my heart I knew I had a higher calling.

While attending the University of Oregon, I landed an internship at *Good Morning America*, and moved to New York to pursue my goal of working in broadcasting. Later, I moved to Los Angeles to work at *Entertainment Tonight*. Even though I had worked for dynamic television shows and was achieving my goals, I wanted to pursue my childhood dream of becoming a singer. It was then that I began to notice changes in my vision. It got harder to track words on the teleprompter, and to see clearly at night. During my twenties, my vision loss seemed to jump almost every other year. When I realized the doctor had been right, that my vision would continue to get worse, I knew I had to become the protector of my dreams. I had to hold onto them, to be the keeper of my own vision.

There is an inner child in all of us with big dreams. I thought, "Even though I can't see very well, I'm still going to make it happen for her." Determined not to let myself down by giving up or settling for less, I made the decision not to let RP hold me back. No matter what the obstacle, I would stay focused. After all, I had promised my inner child I would make her dreams come true!

Even though I couldn't see very well, I never lost my vision of who I wanted to be. As my eyesight got worse, my vision for my life became clearer. Rather than divert from my path,

---

When I realized the doctor had been right, that my vision would continue to get worse, I knew I had to become the protector of my dreams. I had to hold onto them, to be the keeper of my own vision.

I decided to make adjustments for my physical impairment. I wanted to have freedom over my own schedule, so after deep consideration, I transitioned out of the music industry and into a new career in real estate. My first big adjustment to my new mobility challenge was when I decided to give up driving and learn the bus system.

Committed to my clients, I wanted to ensure that my inability to drive did not cause me to skip a beat. It wasn't a matter of *if* I would get around, but *how* I would get around. Taking two to twelve buses to meet with clients meant long days for me. After showing a house, often a million-dollar property, I would watch my clients drive off in their luxury vehicle, and then walk to the bus stop and take two or three buses to get back to the office! I didn't have the traditional image of a glamorous real estate agent, but I was a top producer in Southern California. Why? Because I never let my visual impairment stand in my way, and because I possessed a core confidence rooted in gratitude for all of the opportunities I had been given.

Eventually, I learned that if I couldn't get over it, go under it or get around it on my own, I could find someone who would help me meet the challenge—any challenge. I researched and discovered countless resources for people with visual impairments. And I learned to ask for help. I developed a team of coaches, experts, volunteers and assistants to support me in life and in business. Being forced to delegate turned out to be a blessing, because I didn't get stuck in the common entrepreneurial trap of doing it all.

When people see that I can't see, they really bend over backwards to help me. In having to ask for help, I've seen a different side of people—a generosity, a desire to connect that I cannot describe fully except to say that assisting me is like a gift to them. It gives their lives meaning. It's amazing how much help there is out there, and how many people are willing to participate in the realization of your dream. You don't have to be legally blind to ask for help. You deserve it, whatever your abilities or "disabilities."

Sometimes people adjust to disabilities by downgrading their dreams, their desires and their quality of life. This is their way of "learning to live with it." But why should your life be any less

---

Eventually, I learned that if I couldn't get over it, go under it or get around it on my own, I could find someone who would help me meet the challenge— any challenge.

---

than you want it to be, just because you have a physical challenge? And why would you choose to live a pale imitation of the life you once envisioned, simply because you fear failure, or success, or both?

I made adjustments to make my life bigger, not smaller, and to live the life I had imagined, not a life of compromise and regret. I live full out. No wish is too big and no aim is too high. Today, I travel by myself, domestically and internationally. I hike. I ride a bicycle. I go rollerblading. I love to bowl, and I'm pretty good at it, too. I may have to feel around for the holes, but I play the game. And even though the balls are really hard to see, I play miniature golf. Also, there are benefits to being legally blind: in my world, all my friends are wrinkle-free! And when I look in the mirror,

---

Living full out is really about stepping onto the court and swinging. You won't hit the ball every time, but it's so much better to be on the court playing life full out than to be sitting on the sidelines watching it go by.

---

all I see is beauty and a woman who is proud of who she is. More importantly, my life is richer having gone through this. Don't get me wrong: I wish I could drive, and see people's faces. But I've seen a humanitarian side of people that many don't get to see. And I've become more present, more patient and more confident in my own skin.

Facing a physical challenge can derail even the best-laid plans, but sometimes it has the opposite effect. When I finally accepted that I would lose my vision, I wanted to see and do everything. It was game on! But for many people who *don't* get this type of "wake-up call," life continues to be a struggle, one in which perceived limitations always win.

Sometimes I feel blessed to know that my challenge is physical, because some wounds go much deeper.

I truly believe that we can all become disabled by our fears, insecurities, and doubts. These feelings can be very real for people, and very debilitating. What people need to realize is that they are worth so much more than they are giving themselves credit for, and that life has so much value. Living full out is really about stepping onto the court and swinging. You won't hit the ball every time, but it's so much better to be on the court playing life full out than to be sitting on the sidelines watching it go by.

When the doctor told me I could go blind, he suggested I downsize my dreams and find a different, more "manageable" career. His advice only lit a fire under me to prove him wrong. I've done everything I said I would do, realized every one of my childhood dreams—and I am committed to living my life full out.

Blindness does not define who I am. Don't let your own "disabilities" define who you are, or what you can achieve in life. I don't need 20/20 vision to know that you're beautiful, just the way you are. Whatever is holding you back, whatever flaws you think you cannot get past or obstacles you think you cannot overcome, let my story serve as proof that you *can* and *will* realize your dreams.

Founder of Living Full Out, Nancy Solari is a motivational speaker and life coach who empowers people to overcome the challenges they face and start living the lives of their dreams. Diagnosed with retinitis pigmentosa at age sixteen, Nancy is an authentic example of how you can live the life you want with the right mindset and foundations, regardless of the challenges you face. She achieved her lifelong goals of becoming a reporter and a singer, working for Good Morning America and Entertainment Tonight, and is a successful business owner. Nancy is in her ninth year as a top-producing realtor in Southern California. She recently partnered with the Foundation Fighting Blindness (FFB) to share her inspirational story with others and motivate them to regain their inner vision. To learn more about Nancy, visit www.LivingFullOut.com.

Pregnancy: Miracle or Nightmare

Hannah Bajor

Like so many women for whom having a baby is not a 1-2-3 process, I was told it would take a miracle for me to get pregnant. While I certainly do believe in divine intervention, I knew when I received the hopeless news that I had to find a way to make my own miracle. And I did—not once, not twice, but several times.

Coming from a large Irish family, I never envisioned that getting pregnant would be a challenge. My own mother had eight kids, so I assumed having children was something every woman did naturally, as a part of life. And yet I, the midwife who assisted with this process on a daily basis, could not get pregnant.

For ten long years I struggled with infertility, trying month after month to get that "positive" pregnancy test millions of women yearn for. Finally, at the age of thirty-eight, I got pregnant for the first time. During early pregnancy, I made a conscious decision to be a stay-at-home mom. Like many women, I worried about money, wondering how I was going to be able to afford to give up my high-paying midwifery career.

Sixteen weeks into my pregnancy, tragedy struck, when my little baby growing inside me died. Now I had to be the patient in bed, undergoing a grueling two-day induced labor to deliver my son, who had died inside of me. This pregnancy-loss experience helped me begin to understand the powerful effects one's thoughts, words and actions can have on an unborn child, and on the outcome of one's pregnancy.

After our tremendous loss, my husband and I summoned up the courage to embark on an adventure so many couples take part in today: fertility treatments. I was elated that, for the first time, our insurance would cover the costly procedures.

And I was fully confident that the treatments would work. Six months later, after numerous doctor visits, injections, blood tests, ultrasounds and three failed attempts at intrauterine

---

Sixteen weeks into my pregnancy, tragedy struck, when my little baby growing inside me died.

---

insemination, I decided to try in vitro fertilization (IVF). Then, in the middle of the IVF cycle, I was diagnosed with premature ovarian failure. In other words, I was in premature menopause and no longer producing eggs.

I was promptly removed from the infertility program and informed that I would never have a biological child—unless a miracle happened. My husband and I left the clinic that day in total devastation, thinking all our hopes and dreams of being parents were gone.

I thought, "How could this happen to me, someone who has dedicated my life to helping pregnant women?" What saddened me more was that maybe I was to blame in some small way for losing my one and only opportunity to be a mother, because I had worried about money during my first pregnancy. It seemed the time had come for me to accept that I might be childless. But despite the medical prognosis, deep inside I still felt that one day I would have a child. I knew I had a physical contract to be a parent.

As a midwife, I have delivered thousands of babies and cared for thousands of women before, during and after their pregnancies. Sustaining a head injury while delivering a baby was the catalyst that forced me to walk outside the traditional medical model for pain relief. I then ventured onto the path of holistic healing, obtaining numerous certifications. Even though my chances of becoming pregnant were absolutely zero, I decided to research what I needed to do nutritionally and emotionally to heal my own infertility—I would try to get pregnant on my own. One year later I got pregnant, totally naturally.

When I was twenty-five weeks along, I went into premature labor. The neck of my womb had shortened and opened. I knew that at this stage of my pregnancy, if I delivered the baby, the doctors would be required to resuscitate him. I feared that a baby born at six months' gestation had huge life-threatening

I was promptly removed from the infertility program and informed that I would never have a biological child—unless a miracle happened.

health challenges to face, and a high probability of brain damage. I had to turn the situation around.

Drawing on my energetic healing abilities, I attempted to create balance. I meditated for hours, through the contractions. I called on every power in the universe, every archangel, every master I could think of. I thought, "You have to keep this baby inside me!" After four hours, I stopped the labor and my cervix closed completely, confirmed by ultrasound.

I went on to have a normal, healthy pregnancy, carrying my son to thirty-eight weeks. My miracle baby was born at home, with no complications. Just eight months later another miracle happened—I got pregnant again without even trying, and now I have two healthy boys!

During my second labor I meditated alone, silently embracing each contraction. I was waiting and waiting for ferocious contractions to come and consume my body as they did with my first son—but without warning, I was fully dilated and ready to deliver my baby.

After a little panic and a few phone calls, my midwife, family and friends were there to witness a beautiful, gentle water birth.

Birth is an unpredictable event, and sometimes things go wrong no matter how prepared we are for it. I hemorrhaged badly this second time, losing half my blood volume, but because of expert midwifery management—and an encounter

---

I went on to have a normal, healthy pregnancy, carrying my son to thirty-eight weeks. My miracle baby was born at home, with no complications. Just eight months later another miracle happened—I got pregnant again without even trying, and now I have two healthy boys!

---

with angelic beings—I received another miracle: my own life. I remember hearing my midwife and friends talking to me, but no longer seeing them. What I did see were angelic beings in another world. They were nervous, saying, "Her heartbeat is dropping! We are losing her."

Suddenly I was being shown pictures, clips of my kids' future, images of my family members and friends crying and very upset. I have a very soft heart, and hate to see people crying. So I made a conscious choice to change my death exit-time and stay alive. The angelic beings told me I'd be given another chance at life, so that one day I would bring my midwifery skills—and my knowledge of the energetic dynamics of pregnancy, infertility and miscarriage—to women all over the world.

Hannah Bajor

Traditional medical professionals can look at the pregnancy process from a clinical point of view, but one can't *know* until one has experienced it. Everything I practiced and taught changed once I had given birth myself, because I now have *cellular* knowledge of what women go through. All the traditional education we receive is based on physical anatomy and hormones—but pregnancy is not just a physical process.

Understanding pregnancy, infertility and miscarriage from a higher consciousness has given me a unique perspective from which I now help thousands of women experience the deeper side of pregnancy, honoring themselves as women and the

---

Our thoughts, words and actions have tremendous power and penetrate every physical, mental and emotional cell of mothers' and the babies' bodies.

---

uniqueness of their unborn children. I teach the importance of bonding with your baby's emotions every day; going deep within, walking into the womb emotionally. Because I am a holistic energy healer, I am able to see beyond the physical body and into pregnancy's energy dynamics.

Balancing their energetic systems, much as I did when I went into labor with my first child at twenty-five weeks, women are able to avoid many symptoms of pregnancy. Energy healing can help women overcome infertility and avoid miscarriage and pregnancy complications and the all-too-common Caesarean section. Our thoughts, words and actions have tremendous power and penetrate every physical, mental and emotional cell of mothers' and the babies' bodies. Understanding the energy dynamics of pregnancy gives us the opportunity to heal our own birth-related emotional trauma. It also gives parents-to-be an opportunity to emotionally heal adverse negative thoughts their babies might pick up while in the womb.

My infertility experience gave me a higher understanding regarding the stress and hardship some couples experience in their attempt to achieve a pregnancy.

My heart goes out to all people who have walked the path of infertility. Even if you feel you have exhausted all options, keep searching. Keep trying. Never give up hope. Be open to both traditional and holistic approaches. Do all you can to *create* your own miracles!

Midwife Hannah Bajor, CNM, MSN, RNC, is the author of a highly acclaimed book Birth, A Conscious Choice. *She is the creator of the Lumalove™ line of pregnancy, infertility and miscarriage support-related products and services. Known as the "Pregnancy Super Coach," Hannah is a bridge between traditional and holistic birthing practices.*

Building on almost thirty years as a midwife, in her international telephone healing practice, workshops and speaking engagements, she is a dynamic teacher who captures, informs and empowers her audience. With her unique blend of medical credibility and holistic healing knowledge, Hannah is on the cutting edge of a new era in pregnancy, infertility and miscarriage education. Learn more about Hannah's work at www.LumaLove.com.

Listen to Your Inner Voice

Danny Freedman

The problem with the world today is that there is too much noise. Life is busy and the noise surrounds us from the time we awaken to the time our head hits the pillow at night. The noise isn't confined to the outer world; it invades the mind as well. This is the noise that needs to be silenced. Underneath the roaring waves of the mind are the gentle whisperings of the soul. When we can finally listen to the wisdom of the soul, we begin to live life with integrity and peace.

My story is a real-life example of taking big risks for the sake of quieting the mind and listening to the soul in the midst of a very busy life.

It was the fall of 2007. The company that I helped grow from a local three-person operation to a multinational corporation, operating with over two hundred employees and nine years of quarter-after-quarter growth, was headed for another big expansion. At that time, my wife and I were settling into our brand new house with our two young children who were two and three years old.

Up to this point in my life I had chased after success the best way I knew how. I had created opportunities for myself to grow in the workplace; I had quality relationships with friends and even better relationships with my co-workers. I was well respected in the organization as a person who could be trusted by employees and clients alike. They saw that I had the interests of the people and the company at heart.

With the rapid growth of the company, my role within in it had become very dynamic. I was constantly working out issues in my head, with colleagues, on the phone or on my computer. The job's demands kept me very busy every day, and I was rewarded for my

> *I think all of us have that inner compass. It's a nagging feeling that something isn't right, a feeling that can even be physical. When I am not listening to what my inner voice is telling me, I feel fatigue.*

accomplishments. Finances were great, my family was healthy and well taken care of and I was an executive for an international company before the age of thirty-five. My life was a success, or at least that's what I told myself over and over again.

But something was stirring within me. It began as a subtle feeling of discontent, a faint questioning of my purpose. Over time, the feeling grew and I became aware that I needed to make a drastic change. In other words, the inner voice of my soul was saying "Get out." My inner voice does not, and did not, come to me as an actual voice inside my head. It feels almost like an inner knowing of right and wrong. All through life I have carried a moral compass of some sort. I think all of us have that inner compass. It's a nagging feeling that something isn't right, a feeling that can even be physical. When I am not listening to what my inner voice is telling me, I feel fatigue.

As I look back on my time growing within the corporation, my inner voice was always whispering, trying to give me direction. But when I was in the torrent of building my "successful" life, it seemed too easy to continue to reap the rewards of the material world. Even though I knew in my heart that each day was chipping away at my integrity as I worked primarily for the sake of material gain and nothing more, I felt so busy I couldn't stop long enough to really assess where my life was going.

The physical and emotional signs were there, but I didn't recognize them. I was always exhausted, my body ached, I would get frustrated easily, and more and more I felt like what I was doing made no difference and had no purpose. I acted as if I was really important, but on the inside I often felt insufficient. I began to see others more as a means to an end rather than real people with real problems, goals, strengths and needs. In all of this, I was not outwardly a bad person; I just made the very common mistake of thinking that feeling busy and important is the same as happiness and success.

The busier I got, the more successful I felt—but the less I actually cherished the wonderful people in my life. It was not that I cared for them any less; I just wanted more out of them

---

I went over the cliff with the support and encouragement of my wife, friends and family, which is key. Even unattached people do not need to make major leaps like this alone.

---

because I felt like *I* was giving more. I felt entitled to more respect and more time to work. The busier I got, the more I wanted other people to be busy too. It's a cycle of thinking that I believe a lot of successful people get into.

Also within that cycle of thoughts were all the reasons that I stayed in my unsatisfying career long after I stopped enjoying it. You may recognize some of these noise-makers too: Am I providing my kids with what they need to succeed? Am I taking care of my family? Am I making enough money to retire happy? Are we safe? Am I a good husband? And on and on. The answer to most of these questions is a superficial "Yes," when you are making lots of money. So my work was justified, because I was creating safety and security for my family. But that cycle and that busy-ness were drowning out my inner voice.

There are many strategies to calm the busy mind: meditation, reading, stretching. You have to find what works best for you. Sometimes I simply step out of my office and walk into the backyard to watch nature and accept what is happening right now rather than trying to change it.

In October 2007, my wife bought us two tickets to see Jack Canfield at a fundraising event. The same night that the owners of my company were receiving an entrepreneur award, I was attending a personal growth seminar in another city. That particular night, the choice I was making crystallized. I could continue to live the same life, feeling happy only on the surface, safe in my *not so comfortable* comfort zone, stop growing, and feel less and less zest for life. Or I could take a risk and give myself the opportunity to slow down, appreciate each moment and live in integrity with who I wanted to be and who I truly am.

Within a month, I was out of my career and in search of something more meaningful for my life and work. I heard the whisper of my soul, saying there was something more for me to do. I jumped off the cliff and took a risk which propelled me into real life, leaving the illusion of success behind. I jumped into a life without blinders on, where people are honest with me and I am willing to listen and where I no longer feel like I am just reacting to whatever confronts me, hoping to make it through.

I went over the cliff with the support and encouragement of my wife, friends and family, which is key. Even unattached people do not need to make major leaps like this alone. As my career ended, I had no plans for what to do next. I took some time to simply *be* for a while, and found that I had actually been missing out on a lot of the richness in life. Through this process, I learned about what really matters to me.

This is not a story of immediate liberation and a straight line to the top of the next ladder of success, but rather of recognition that I am now on the path I want to be on. I am taking the time to develop my greatest assets as someone who sees the strengths of others and helps them to see those strengths in themselves. I see the value of exploring my own strengths and becoming aware of my shortcomings. As a result, I think I am becoming a better father, spouse, son, brother, friend and world citizen. I am immersed in the richness of daily living.

It is easy for me to appreciate the little moments with my children and wife, to notice the helpfulness of strangers and the goodness in people who are trying to heal the world and take consciousness to a new level. I still have struggles with breaking old habits and creating new ones. Sometimes I catch myself ploughing through work in the old mentality of just trying to get things done, but as I have discovered what it is like to slow

---

It is inspiring to know, when I wake up in the morning, that I am living in truth and sincerity all of the time. I am living each day with reverence, and meaning is found in every corner of my life.

---

down and live in integrity everyday, I feel so much more alive. It is inspiring to know, when I wake up in the morning, that I am living in truth and sincerity all of the time. I am living each day with reverence, and meaning is found in every corner of my life.

I continue to learn valuable lessons along the way. The soul is always sharing its wisdom. If you stop to quiet the mind and listen, you will hear it whispering. We have been training ourselves to focus on the physical world for so long that we forget we are only here for a small—but not insignificant—fragment of time. Your soul, or inner voice, has infinite wisdom to guide you.

I have learned how important it is to recognize the subtle signs that I'm in trouble, before it is too late. I have learned how important it is to be a student in life, always learning, and to be mindful of the choices I am making every day. I have learned that the more you head down this road, the more angels show up to help you find your way. Lastly, I have learned that the only way anyone will come to understand who they are, why they are here and where they are going is by slowing down long enough to find out.

For nine years, Danny Freedman helped build a small local foreign exchange company into a multinational corporation. When he left, Danny was Vice President in charge of global business development. He is now a personal and business coach, dedicated to helping others take the little and big risks they need to live more inspired, joyful lives. Danny is the founder of Evolution Coaching, offering a variety of workshops and seminars for individuals and businesses. He also offers "Inspiration Now! The 30-Day Challenge," an excellent program for discovering the inspiration you can be in the world. For more information about Danny and his programs, go to www.DannyFreedman.com.

Speaking for the Last in Line

Alison Sawyer Current

My home is on the small island of Isla Mujeres, Mexico. It is one of the most beautiful places on earth—and one of the most troubling. From my window, I can see the ocean, surrounding me on three sides.

But, when we first arrived, I could also see skinny, mangy dogs wandering the streets and the beaches anywhere I looked. Malnourished, sick, neglected, abused or stalked by untrained dogcatchers with mobile generators rigged for brutal, instant electrocutions, these dogs have no one to look out for them—except me. So I've become their semi-official spokesperson, known around the island and beyond as "the dog lady." My house became "puppy camp."

My husband Jeff and I moved here from Boulder, Colorado, about ten years ago. We'd visited a few times and fallen in love with the place—and when we found a gorgeous piece of property for sale, we found a way to buy it. I'd been a pretty successful potter for thirty years, and figured I could work just as well in Mexico. Our kids had all graduated and we were ripe for a change.

If you are somebody who notices animals, the first thing you would have seen getting off the ferry on Isla Mujeres—at that time—was the dog situation. Packs of wild dogs roamed the beaches, searching for food. Domestic dogs weren't in much better shape. They were everywhere, like friendly flea- and tick-ridden derelicts.

As we struggled through the trials of building our house, I couldn't help but notice that most of the people here, who struggle for their own survival and have different attitudes about domestic animals, were not caring for their cats and

---

I couldn't stand by and just watch this stuff happen.

---

dogs. Wild dogs were pests that were periodically rounded up and exterminated for fear they would scare off the tourists. The so-called "pets" were left mostly to fend for themselves as they continued to breed two litters a year, adding to the enormous population of neglected animals already in the streets. Puppies were routinely abandoned in dumps, empty lots and garbage cans—and left to die.

I couldn't stand by and just watch this stuff happen. So at first I did a few small rescue operations with other people. Then I helped out at a spay and neuter clinic with a couple of friends, Americans who had a little bookstore. These ladies had been fostering groups of puppies at the store in an effort to get them adopted by tourists. (Jordie, the sweet puppy they'd adopted from the street, had been carted off in a roundup and electrocuted the same day, before they could claim her.) Little kids loved to visit, and there were some successful adoptions. But there were so many puppies that the store had begun to smell, people were complaining and their business was suffering.

So I said, "Look, I've got this room over my garage I'm not using for anything. I'll take the puppies, nurse them back to health and when they're ready, I'll bring them back to the store where people can see them and adopt them." That was my first real foray into animal rescue—with seventeen beautiful little pups who have since been adopted into loving, forever homes.

My house became known as "puppy camp," and from then on, I've always had rescue dogs. Eventually the ladies had to close their store and I was *it* on Isla Mujeres. People brought me strays, the puppies kept on coming and we just rolled with it.

I didn't have a vision for this work; I just couldn't say no. Because I really cared, though I really didn't know what I was doing and I had no formal training, groups coming in to do spay and neuter clinics helped me. They'd give me medical advice and expired medicines and counsel me on how to deal with behavioral problems. But I didn't have a clue. Jeff and I built our first kennel out of old doors! And the number of dogs kept increasing. I'd have thirty, forty of them at once.

Gradually, our house became a sort of tourist site. Anybody who was interested in animals knew I was there—all they had to do was ask for the "dog lady" and anybody in town could point them in the right direction. They came to bring donations, or walk the dogs or just to talk about how upset they felt about the dogs they'd seen. During tourist season I'd have several visits a day. This resulted in some very happy adoptions, and formed a support group of sorts.

Isla Mujeres has a way of getting under your skin; some of our tourist friends return year after year. They follow my website and read my newsletters, and some come to volunteer with spay and neuter clinics.

Two of them, a lovely young couple named Maia and Matt, fell in love with a sweet Schnauzer mix and presented him to Matt's mom for Christmas a few years ago. Since then, Matt and Maia have created Petprojectrescue.com in Minneapolis specifically to bring Isla dogs to loving homes in the U.S. I can't tell you how amazing it is to get a photo of a plump, happy puppy sprawled on a couch—remembering that, when he came to me, he was starving, sick and bald. There's absolutely nothing better.

In the past couple of years I've found many wonderful rescue organizations to work with that will take our Isla dogs and find loving, forever homes for them in the US and Canada. Over time, I've gathered more and more support from amazing, dedicated people who come down to Isla to do spay and neuter clinics and generously answer all my questions. Thank goodness for their practical *and* moral support, because this road has not always been easy.

There have been a few islanders who have threatened to deport me and kill my dogs, and have managed to poison some (if a dog wants to jump a fence, he will find a way). The authorities—whose trucks I try to follow after roundups to

---

I can't tell you how amazing it is to get a photo of a plump, happy puppy sprawled on a couch— remembering that, when he came to me, he was starving, sick and bald. There's absolutely nothing better.

---

save the dogs they are planning to electrocute—have switched to portable generators so they can kill as many dogs as possible before I can find them. As the only one caring for the dogs, I'm somehow held accountable for *all* the dogs on the island, and blamed when any dog damages property or bites someone. And I still have broken windows after Hurricane Wilma, because my money and time literally go to the dogs!

Even with the hard stuff, I feel like the luckiest person alive. All I want to do is this. It's heartbreaking, at times; I've had whole litters of sick puppies die in my arms. But I do see a difference. There are fewer dogs on the street. Sometimes I see people walking them! And they bring them to me now, rather than just dumping them somewhere. Even if I'm overcrowded,

I'm thrilled when that happens, because the animals have a chance and I know the attitude here is changing. It means that people finally care enough to bring their animals somewhere they know they'll be taken care of. That's huge.

I'm lucky, too, to have a wonderful husband who loves me dearly and keeps me grounded and coming up for air. Sometimes he gets frustrated, of course, and says, "What are we going to

---

It's okay not to have a plan. Just go ahead, and things unfold. You just find a way. It makes you adaptable, and open to anything.

DO?" I say, "Don't ask me that!" Because I don't *have* an answer. And I'm glad I don't. If I'd thought things through when I took those first seventeen puppies in, I *wouldn't* have done it. As of this writing, we've found homes for thousands of dogs. If I had asked that question and needed an answer, those dogs would be dead. Two thousand dogs—that's pretty cool! *That* keeps me going.

It's okay not to have a plan. Just go ahead, and things unfold. You just find a way. It makes you adaptable, and open to anything. I found that to do something that seems insurmountable, I had to make a rule for myself that I would never pass an animal that was in desperate shape without trying to help. For my cause, it can be the littlest thing, like bringing dog food in the car and feeding hungry guys as I find them, or putting a collar on a stray. So start small. Make a rule for yourself that you have to follow. Don't try to get to the end of the problem, just do something every day to try to make a difference. It's about a consistent effort. But do make that rule. If you miss it occasionally, it doesn't mean you're a bad person. Just start again the next day.

As for us, we're now raising money for the most essential piece of this work: a mobile spay, neuter and vaccination clinic.

Of course, we'll keep on rescuing puppies and dogs, and finding them great homes. We'll keep doing this work, little by little, day by day, because we love it—and because we are the ones who have appeared, in the right place and at this time, to speak for our friends who cannot speak.

Soon after moving to Isla Mujeres, Mexico in 1999, Alison Sawyer Current became involved with animal rescue efforts there. She and her husband Jeff have since started an unofficial humane society for the island along with a website, www.IslaAnimals.org, to raise awareness and funds. They take in any animal in need, tend to its health, vaccinate, spay and socialize—and then find a loving forever home whenever possible. The net proceeds from Alison's novel, No Urn for the Ashes *and her new novel,* The Dog Lady of Mexico, *benefit Isla Animals. Charlie Sawyer, Alison's son, is at work on* Last in Line, *a documentary about the animals of Isla Mujeres and Alison's work.*

Sixty Seconds to Physical Freedom

Donald W. Kipp

This past Memorial Day weekend, I was scheduled to give a public lecture in California. A female veteran of the Gulf War had been in contact with me over the phone, telling me how she hoped she could attend. She had suffered multiple traumas in her service and several more since: she had a brain injury and PTSD; couldn't stand normally and walked with shuffling steps, a cane and a great deal of pain. When she lay down, her feet bent forward dramatically. It was an hour-and-a-half-long drive for her to get to my lecture.

Through incredible fortitude, she did make it to the lecture. She arrived very weepy and emotional, in a great deal of physical and mental pain. I called her forward, and after I'd worked on her for a few seconds without even touching her, she stood up tall. Her face had completely changed. She was smiling. All the grief she'd been feeling had been lifted, and she could stand steadily without pain. The audience, many with mouths open, watched this profound transformation. It took less than sixty seconds.

Then I put her on the table. I worked on her head and neck, never below her waist, and her feet released and moved to a normal position. The audience saw that and reacted, so she looked down at her feet and was dumbfounded. "Oh, my God," she said. "Look at my feet." What amazed her was not only that she had healed, but that it happened so quickly and effortlessly. The audience, too, was stunned. To some it seemed like a miracle, and perhaps in some way it was—but it was also a modality that required years of study, development and practice before one moment of application.

What I used that day I named Neuroenergetic Release™ (NER), because it uses the neurological and energetic control systems of the body to release imbalance. I call it relational medicine because it is based in all the physical relationships of our bodies, the relationships between all levels of our existence, and how we relate to the rest of the universe.

Quantum physics basically says that everything in the universe is interconnected. Everything affects everything, and what we see as solids or particles are, in fact, energy. NER holds that most symptoms we experience result from core-distortion patterns— imbalances, contractions and patterns of compensation that are stored throughout the entire body. Core-distortion patterns develop after trauma or injury, and sometimes are the result of the birth process itself. These patterns worsen over time and surface as a variety of symptoms later in life—back pain, neck and shoulder pain, breathing problems, digestive problems. The patterns exist on the physical, energetic and emotional planes, and are the root of almost all bodily pain and dysfunction. And because all these planes are connected, when patterns change on one level, they change on all levels.

I haven't always practiced NER; but, reflecting, I can see that in some way I was always working towards it. I became interested in manual therapies and alternative medicine after I experienced their healing effects following my own serious back injury. In college, I studied a pre-med curriculum, but became disillusioned by the limited, compartmentalized view of health so prevalent in Western medicine.

My epiphany for NER came in 1992. At the time, I was practicing manual therapy and structural body work with more traditional therapies. My client was a gentleman in his early sixties who had multiple ruptured discs and was in a lot of pain. While working on him, I decided to bring together many elements I knew from different systems—energy, anatomy, form and function, breathing, what I sensed with my hands—into treating him.

> The patterns exist on the physical, energetic and emotional planes, and are the root of almost all bodily pain and dysfunction. And because all these planes are connected, when patterns change on one level, they change on all levels.

After forty-five minutes, he went from being hunched over in an "old man" posture to standing up straight like a twenty-year old Marine—and was out of pain. I knew I'd stumbled upon something profound.

I came to realize that I was able to see relationships in the body, mind and spirit that no one else had identified. Some relationships are consistent among all people, but everyone has individual patterns, and understanding those patterns is key. What led to this becoming such a powerful system was my recognition that this was truly an illuminating discovery, and that every patient had something to teach me.

People often ask, "What is NER like?" or, "How is it different?" The short answer is that is it isn't like anything, and what's different is how quick, easy and profound the results are. One of my gifts is to look at the physical body and not only see relationships, but also *feel* them. Another gift is, I can teach this to others. Using NER, one can quickly look at someone and see if he is better or if something helped him. We can always objectively measure if something is helpful, if change is positive and if we are on the right track.

I know there are many powerful modalities that effect many powerful healings. But in over twenty years of searching, I haven't seen anything else that helps such a variety of people with such varied conditions as profoundly, as quickly and as consistently as Neuroenergetic Release™. So maybe one of its

---

Some people have called me a healer, but I resist that title. I give the body new information with which to change, and the body heals itself.

---

most powerful attributes is that it is an organized system that is highly replicable and teachable. NER works, in part, because of the physical relationships it recognizes in our bodies. We can lay out anatomical and physiological explanations for that. But the energetic aspect comes down to quantum physics: everything is affected by everything and everything is energy.

Some people have called me a healer, but I resist that title. I give the body new information with which to change, and the body heals itself. There is only one true healer, and that is the body itself. Maybe a more powerful title is teacher—whether I am giving an individual's body information on how to heal itself or giving an NER practitioner information on how to heal others.

NER impacts the health of patients, and sometimes even their life direction. One client was given an epidural during childbirth, and she emerged with low back pain, lower extremity pain and "anxiety attacks." She couldn't walk normally, and she'd tried so many remedies that the medical world had written her off. After one brief NER session, she walked out pain-free, with a normal gait, calmly proceeding straight to a store where she bought a pair of non-orthopedic shoes for the first time in four years. She is now completing her prerequisites so she can study Neuroenergetic Release™.

I occasionally encounter skepticism: that's quite natural, given the novelty of NER. With all clients and patients, we stop after the first one-to-sixty seconds of treatment to give them the physical experience of change. Then we reevaluate the situation given their experience of a physical shift, and the lessening of pain or discomfort. I do this to give them a knowing, to help change their paradigm so that they are more willing to participate in what they may have previously thought impossible.

Everything we have been taught, someone—at some time—just made up. That doesn't mean it's true; but the minute a person says something is or isn't true, he stops learning in that area. Quantum physics also teaches us that we are the observers in our own realities, and we can determine our realities. But in order to change ourselves, we have to change the paradigms

---

In my practice and in my public speaking I try to get people to say, "Maybe." Willingness comes in varying degrees, but the minute someone says, "Maybe," he's open to more possibilities.

---

in which we operate that are *preventing* change. In my practice and in my public speaking I try to get people to say, "Maybe." Willingness comes in varying degrees, but the minute someone says, "Maybe," he's open to more possibilities.

My own paradigm is, "Healing is easy, it doesn't have to hurt, and results are going to be quick and long-lasting." That paradigm has allowed me to help thousands. As the whole world adopts more powerful paradigms, anything is truly possible.

We often see scoliosis (a curve in the spine) among teenagers and others in great physical pain who've been told that they need rods in their backs, or to wear braces for years. In one or two NER sessions, they're out of pain—without surgery or a brace—and they're two inches taller because their spines have straightened. Scoliosis patients in their fifties, sixties and seventies who have endured distressing pain their entire lives become pain-free in a matter of days.

Carpal Tunnel Syndrome (CTS) is the number one occupational injury. Companies spend approximately thirty thousand dollars per case. NER can resolve that issue in a few sessions with no work lost and no surgery. NER can even predict and prevent CTS; with a quick look at a client we can see the imbalances that lead to it.

And because NER balances the core patterns that, when released, allow the body to heal itself, maintenance to stay well or at optimum performance usually entails just one or two visits a year. In my wellness practice, I feel great joy and gratitude in having helped so many people so profoundly. And I am grateful for being, for lack of a better expression, a *channel* for this information to have come through. Now it can be taught to others who can in turn touch thousands, maybe even millions, of other lives. Again, the body is the only healer. What happened with that veteran on that Memorial Day Weekend can happen for anyone, and just as fast, because everyone has a body that wants to heal—even you. It's just waiting for the right information, and for you to say, "Maybe."

Donald W. Kipp is the inventor and founder of Neuroenergetic Release Wellness System™, which consistently helps people experience pain relief, greater health and optimum performance--in seconds. He has practiced natural health care, natural pain relief and bio-structural therapy for over twenty years, helping thousands gain physical freedom and even, literally, be taller. NER continues to evolve, and Don remains open to learning what truths all healing has in common.

Don has taught Neuroenergetic Release™ to health professionals since 1994. Please visit www.Body-Awareness.com to learn more about Don and NER.

Claim Your Birthright

Donna Aazura

All of us are deeply influenced by our childhood experiences. And we now know that between birth and age six, children are especially impressionable, programmable and receptive; every message they take in goes straight to the subconscious and is stored in a file marked "fact and truth." As adults, we may not realize that the beliefs we formed in early childhood are deeply embedded in our subconscious and are still busy shaping our lives.

For me, it's been a journey of profound discovery to finally release the core beliefs that kept me separate from my authentic self. Like so many others, I didn't receive all positive messages in my most impressionable years. Hearing negative messages, I stored them in my subconscious as the truth. Then, as an adult, I couldn't understand why I was attracting the opposite of what I said I wanted. I had done extensive work on myself—focused, set goals, made vision boards, meditated and studied various healing modalities. So why did the life I wanted still elude me?

What I didn't know at the time was that the underlying negative beliefs I held about myself and the world around me were running my life. What I attracted, because of what I believed to be true, showed up as an abusive marriage, struggles with money and a continuing sense of low self esteem. "There's something wrong with me," "I'm not valuable," "I should be different than I am." These are not unusual programs for the mind to run. And when we work on ourselves through cognitive therapy, we can arrive at a point where we're able to logically assert to ourselves that the mind-chatter isn't true. Sometimes acknowledging that it isn't true is enough; however, most people still fall back into some form of negative self-talk.

Your outer world is always a reflection of your inner reality. If you are attracting situations that aren't serving you or allowing you to move forward in your life, as I was, there is likely a program running that believes that's how things should be. I realized for myself that I had to change on the inside in order for my life to shift. But it took a while for me to discover the tools for lasting change.

In 1986, as a single mom with four children, I had a near-death experience. For about two weeks beforehand, I had a deep intuition that I was going to die. There was no reason for it; nothing was wrong with me. But mentally, I was saying goodbye to my children. Then I had a very minor medical procedure and

---

As adults, we may not realize that the beliefs we formed in early childhood are deeply embedded in our subconscious and are still busy shaping our lives.

---

almost died in the process. I woke up afterward and everything was different. For a few weeks I just sat in a state of utter bliss, feeling complete peace. For the first time, I knew there was something much bigger at work in my life.

Even after that near-death experience, some of my negative subconscious programs were still running. I returned to fear, lack and dissatisfaction. A year later, I developed a large tumor. I chose not to pursue traditional medical treatment because I had a very strong sense that I had somehow created it. It became clear to me I was one-hundred-percent responsible for my own life and what I chose to do with it. I knew that to get to the other side I had to un-create the illness myself.

I knew that God did not create me to struggle and suffer as I had. I felt guided to focus my intention, really looking at the emotional pain I had taken on. I decided to forgive myself, accept

---

It became clear to me I was one-hundred-percent responsible for my own life and what I chose to do with it.

---

my experiences and realize I was not any of the erroneous labels I'd slapped on myself through programming. To my doctors' astonishment, the tumor dissolved.

This was a huge awakening for me. To me, the tumor represented my self-destruction. And that's not what I came here to do. To find I had the power to make that choice was profound.

Subsequently, I left the corporate world to study how the subconscious mind works, and how we create our lives. I eventually ended up working as a medical hypnotherapist. I discovered I was very good at hypnotherapy; but, like cognitive therapy, it worked only some of the time. I wanted to see quicker, lasting changes for my clients. There has to be a way, I thought, that we can access subconscious programming, find what it really is that's keeping us stuck and just clear it instantly. Now, that's what I do.

Over time in my practice, I developed Awareness Effect™ (AE), a system for quickly identifying and clearing unsupportive beliefs. Using a technique known as muscle testing, my clients and I can determine which limiting beliefs are running. To start, I listen to a client speak about himself, how he feels stuck, and which issues continue to cycle through his life. Then we make statements based on those beliefs and test them using muscle testing: "I'm not worthy." "I'm supposed to suffer." "Love is pain."

When we discover a belief that is not serving him, we come to an agreement to delete it (we cannot clear a belief without a client's consent). Then, from a place of energetic information that comes from both the client and the source, we delete the

---

When we possess a deeper sense of self-love and acceptance because of it, inner peace comes.

---

belief instantly. If the belief won't clear, there is a core belief underneath it that must be discovered and cleared. We just keep going till we get to it. And when we do, the house of cards finally falls.

AE has been profound for my clients. One woman who had suffered a stroke for which there was no medical explanation came to me, suffering from a deep fear that it would happen to her again. We actually identified a core belief from her childhood that she could get loving attention only if she were sick. After clearing, she had no more headaches, panic or fear, but instead a deep knowing that she would be fine. "I've got my life back," she told me. She attracts different experiences, and has let go of replaying the story that sickness is somehow required of her—because her subconscious triggers are gone.

In my practice, I've worked with several people who are children of Depression-era parents. These clients generally want more out of life, and have great skills, but tend to hit a ceiling when it comes to money. When I test them, lack and fear of loss show up so great that without knowing it, they are sabotaging themselves. They often carry a lot of guilt, because they feel responsible for their parents' struggles. The fear and guilt stop them from being successful. We clear the beliefs they've taken on from their parents (pinch every penny, work, work, work) so they can relax and make room for abundance.

Beliefs around relationships surface a lot in this work. A gentleman recently came into my office; he wanted to start dating again after a failed marriage, but was terrified. He held the belief that he would be betrayed and abandoned by any woman with whom he was involved. We discovered he was running this program because his mother had left home when he was a small child. His deep fear of abandonment also led to the destruction of his first marriage. After one session, we cleared the belief that all women would leave him. He's now dating and very happy.

At first, the speed of change in my clients' lives seemed remarkable. But then I realized it didn't have to be. Why should there be a time requirement for healing? Why should we slog and struggle? Shift can happen instantly. And when it does, there's no time to judge the belief; we just change it.

What I discovered allowed me and many other individuals to experience our own authenticity. When we possess a deeper sense of self-love and acceptance because of it, inner peace comes. We can then view ourselves, and the world, from a more compassionate place—and claim our divine birthright as truly

---

Take the triggers away and peace settles in. Forgiveness becomes easy, compassion plentiful.

---

connected, authentic beings. I, for example, not only cleared my tumor, but also changed my core beliefs, which has positively influenced every corner of my life. I am in good health, and I am blessed to have an incredible marriage. A deep sense of purpose runs through my life, and I feel I have found my birthright, my right place in the Universe.

You are an integral part of the puzzle. As you find inner peace and personal fulfillment, the very quantum field soaks up your positive influence and spreads it to everything else in existence. All you need is life mastery tools to support your new belief structures.

So this work has naturally become the cornerstone of the New Human Project™, an organization dedicated to positively influencing world peace. Its role is to bring authenticity, peace and oneness to the global community. We know when we come back to the truth of who we really are, the triggers that create our anger, fear and judgments will start to fade, and we will be able to recognize our oneness with all life. Take the triggers away and peace settles in. Forgiveness becomes easy, compassion plentiful. Which is how life is meant to be, for each of us individually—and for all of us as one.

A leading expert on consciousness, Donna Aazura is the developer of the Awareness Effect™ system, designed to quickly identify unsupportive beliefs and clear them instantly so clients can live the life they deserve. Donna has inspired thousands of people to live a more joyful, authentic life. She believes it is everyone's divine right to know and embody their life purpose, to feel physically good, to be successful, to have financial abundance and to feel fulfilled. Her mission is evolutionary consciousness, creating a radical shift on a global scale to secure life on earth.

Donna's background as a spiritual counselor and coach, a Certified Medical Hypnotherapist and an ordained minister, has given her more than twenty years' experience in personal and group facilitation. She delivers power-packed presentations on self worth, inner peace, abundance and relationships. Donna is CEO and founder of the New Human Project™, an organization dedicated to expanding human consciousness and manifesting world peace. To learn more about Donna visit www.DonnaAazura.com.

Getting to the Dance

Liz Wilder

Today, my life is literally filled with dancing. It is also filled with happiness, serenity, hard work, freedom, wonderful children and an incredible husband. It's my dancing, though, that symbolizes the joy that is my life. But it hasn't always been this way. To get to the dance that is my life, I had to endure so many painful hardships that I know many other women encounter. And everything I needed to know to overcome those obstacles I learned as a little girl, working in the fish markets of Manila in the Philippines.

I was born in Manila, the last of five children. When I was one year old, my father abandoned our family, and though my mother worked very hard, she could not afford to raise us five children by herself. So she sent us all to stay with different aunts and uncles, and over the next sixteen years I lived in many different localities throughout Manila, usually with relatives.

It was my Aunt Victoria, also my godmother, who introduced me to the fish market. Around three in the morning, my aunt and her partner drove to the wholesalers to buy their fish. Then they headed to the market, where they sold fish from seven in the morning until nine at night. My aunt would not get home until ten, and then early the next day, at three in the morning, she started the routine all over again. I have always been a very hard worker, and that's because of the work ethic my aunt and mother instilled in me. I believe that if you keep working hard, something will eventually turn up; but more importantly, I believe hard work develops self-worth, something many women unfortunately lack.

I was ten years old and in the fourth grade when I started helping my aunt at the fish market. The market was busiest from nine until noon, and in the evening from five until about eight-thirty. During those crucial times, fish sellers had to attract buyers using different selling techniques. My technique was to yell, "We have the best fresh fish here! Cheap over here!" It may have not been a dazzling technique, but it was uniquely mine, and it was effective in part because I was so persistent with it.

I believe that if you keep working hard, something will eventually turn up; but more importantly, I believe hard work develops self-worth, something many women unfortunately lack.

Persistence is so key in this world. Just because something doesn't work nine times doesn't mean I shouldn't try it a tenth time. It may be that tenth time that it finally works.

Eventually I returned home to my mother, who was also a fish vendor, and I helped her, too. She allowed me to handle the financial transactions at the market. That is when I learned how to be very quick and nimble at adding and subtracting in my head, and at transacting business. If I made a mistake in giving back too much change, that was profit lost. Profit wasn't just about money; it was also about my time, my worth. One day, working alone, I sold a lot of fish; but I sold them at a cheap price, and at the end of the day I realized I'd made only a few pesos profit. My mother told me I needed to stop selling fish so cheaply. My time was more valuable than that. My work was more valuable than that. I was more valuable than that. And if I didn't place a higher value on my work, on me, no one else would.

All of these lessons were learned in order for me to embark upon a life that was going to bring more hardship than I'd already endured—more hardship than I could imagine. But there was one more lesson I was going to need to get me through, one I didn't learn at the fish market, and that was the lesson of learning to

---

We need to turn all of our problems into challenges that motivate us to keep moving on. Never give up!

---

put my faith in God. I was raised to know right from wrong, and to know that if you did something wrong it would come back to haunt you. More importantly, I was raised to believe in a God who would give me the strength to endure whatever came my way, if only I believed in Him and relied on Him enough.

I attended college through a scholarship. Of course, this wasn't without its own set of challenges. You see, my father, who had returned home when I was ten, was adamantly opposed to a girl attending college. Making babies and being a good wife was all I should expect from my life, according to him. But his opinion simply did not matter to me.

I married my first husband, probably more as an escape from my father than for true love, and a year later I gave birth to my daughter, Marygrace. My alcoholic husband began abusing me, and then abandoned my very young daughter and me. Heartbroken but hopeful, I went on with my life. I continued working hard and even attended law school for two and a half years. We all have problems in life. It's important for us not to get worked up by the little ones, and also to pick ourselves up after being knocked down by the big ones. We need to turn all of our problems into challenges that motivate us to keep moving on. Never give up!

While I was in law school, a fellow student who was a good friend and also a single mother suggested we respond to an advertisement looking for wives for military men in the United States. I did respond, and on October 15, 1985, at the age of twenty-eight, I left law school and immigrated with my daughter

---

I needed to be living a life of positive energy in order to believe I deserved the positive energy of his life, his love.

---

to Orange County, California, where I married a Marine sergeant. Little did I know, he was also an alcoholic. After a year and a half of marriage, he, too, began to abuse me terribly. Because I was in America, a vast new place I still didn't understand, I was too frightened to leave. We lived on base, and because military houses are so close to each other, my neighbors heard the constant abuse. One neighbor told me, "If you need to leave, I can give you the name and address of a battered woman's shelter."

On one particular Sunday afternoon, my husband was very drunk. He threw me down on the kitchen floor and began choking me. I was flopping around like a fish, trying to survive. After my father had returned home, I watched him abuse my mother for years. I couldn't understand how my mother, who'd taught me how to value myself, didn't value herself more. Years of hard work had instilled a self-worth in me that I wasn't about to let be beaten out. I knew I deserved better. Staying with my husband was cheapening my worth, my time and myself. I was the fish, and I was underselling me.

Too many women remain in abusive relationships because they simply don't realize that they deserve better. They do deserve better, but they have to believe that in order to pursue what's better. I escaped and moved into the women's shelter in Laguna Beach with Marygrace and my young son, Joe, the one blessing from that second marriage. At the shelter, someone said, "A restaurant in town needs someone to water plants." I took the job. Despite my education, my college degree, I wasn't too proud. I was willing to work anywhere to support my children and me. I was in survival mode.

Over the next years, I had so many jobs. For various reasons, every eleven months I had to get a new one. I still kept moving forward, though sometimes I was overcome with despair. In the middle of the night I would cry and pray for life to get better. But no matter how hard I cried, when morning came around I got up and went to work. I did what I needed to do, and my faith helped sustain me.

Eventually, I got a temporary job in a law office where my two and half years in law school served me well. After a while, that office offered me a full-time, permanent job. I was overjoyed. All those previous jobs had been like the nine times I kept shouting, "We have the best fresh fish here." And the job in the law office was like the tenth time I shouted. It was the reward for my persistence.

The key was this: I stopped letting myself be a victim. Terrible things had happened to me, yes, but when you're a victim, you give your tormentors power over you. When you're not a victim, you take away their power and learn to rely on your own power. And eventually, through perseverance (that word again), I started to achieve my dreams. I saved enough money to buy my own house. My daughter went to college and earned a four-year degree. My son, Joe, received a full university scholarship and is expected to complete his master's degree in computer science this school year. My life kept filling up with positive energy. And just when I thought it couldn't get much better, along came Ron.

I met Ron at a West Coast Swing dance convention in Monterey, California. We both love dancing. Some years before, I'd taken up ballroom and swing dancing as a hobby, and it is now one of my passions. It is also a part-time vocation: Ron and I teach dancing in our home.

I firmly believe that Ron is the person I'm meant to be with in this world. But had he come along sooner in my life, I wouldn't have been ready for him. I needed to be living a life of positive energy in order to believe I deserved the positive energy of his life, his love. To some, my life now may seem bland, but it is anything but that to me. I wake up, and I'm happy, and I tell my husband I'm glad to be with him. I drink my morning coffee and pray to the Lord, thanking Him for my safety. I have two grown, healthy children; I have a very good job; I am involved in many community organizations and I dance, often and joyously. My life is a dance!

And I also have a new dream, which I am working to fulfill. I'm working very hard to let as many women as possible know that no matter how difficult their lives may be, all they have to do is find a way to use what they know to improve their lives and the lives of their children. In other words, I'm working to empower other women to get to their dance.

Liz Wilder lives in Reno, Nevada, with her husband, Ron. She is currently working for the United States government. She's also an avid ballroom and West Coast Swing dancer; she has won several competitions and teaches classes with her husband. Liz is dedicated to helping children and women overcome their obstacles in order to live more fulfilling, happy lives, as she had to, and her full story can be read in her forthcoming book, The Girl in the Fish Market. *To learn more about Liz, visit www. GirlInTheFishMarket.com.*

See It, Say It, Make It So

Julie Ann Cohn

I've experienced quite a ride in this life. Over twenty-five years as a successful marketing executive, over eleven years as a healer, and after three near-death experiences, the third of which was completely profound and life altering, I have learned that there is a simple formula that will help each and every one of us overcome—and achieve—absolutely anything: See it, say it, make it so.

This sounds deceptively simple, but it's a formula that has succeeded for me time and time again, through every challenge and opportunity I've faced in this life. It really works; it's like a magic spell.

And it's a formula we understand and follow as children, without even knowing it. Kids use it when they play "let's pretend." For a little kid, being a cowboy is as easy as deciding he wants to be a cowboy. He sets an intention without being aware that's what he's doing; he just accomplishes it naturally. Then he says to his friends, "We're playing cowboys!" and proceeds to play the game.

It may not seem to be quite so easy for us adults, with all our various blocks, habits and inhibitions. But we're still capable of using the formula. In fact, the formula is basic, instinctive. It's encoded in our DNA. Our survival as a species has always been based on our ability to adapt and problem-solve at a fundamental level. Throughout the ages, humans have recognized challenging or opportune situations, made decisions accordingly, communicated their decisions and then taken action to survive and even thrive. The formula is one with the greatest of human challenges: to look within and take responsibility for our own lives. We are in control of our own bodies, brains and choices.

Thanks in part to my mom, a wonderful role model, I learned at a young age that everything I did in my life was my own choice. This gave me a sense of both great freedom and great responsibility. I knew that not everything that occurred was under my control, but that I could choose my *response* to any

> The formula is one with the greatest of human challenges: to look within and take responsibility for our own lives. We are in control of our own bodies, brains and choices.

situation. For me, this is still the definition of free will. What we truly need is to realize that through free will, our faith and whatever external and higher powers we choose to connect with, we can pull through anything. If we trust in that, we can trust in our own ability to see it, say it, and make it so.

I am a case in point. During my twenty-five years as a top advertising/database marketing executive, I became known as an innovator and an expert. Working for major advertising agencies, I created programs for Disney, the Pepsi Bottle Cap game, the first database for McDonald's and Toyota's local store loyalty marketing program. I was on the team that created the American Airlines Frequent Flyer program. I experienced great success through using the formula, letting it drive and inspire my work instead of being bogged in traditional ways of thinking that may not have benefited my clients or generated great ideas.

Julie Ann Cohn

People tend to draw distinctions between their lives and their businesses, not realizing that the tools for success are identical in each. But in truth, the "see it, say it, make it so" formula works its magic equally in both the personal and the professional realms of our lives.

I learned the importance of this firsthand in 1998, when, at the height of my career in advertising and marketing, I was involved in a terrible car accident. Driving down Los Angeles's Southbound 405 freeway in my Corvette, I was struck by a hit-and-run driver. Somehow, my brakes, seatbelt and airbag all failed, and I spun out of control, crashing head-on into the concrete divider. My spine was permanently damaged, my back broken, my stomach lacerated. Three fingers of my left hand had been severed. The doctors said I would never recover, never walk normally, never be off medication or live without pain.

Recovery was very difficult. I had over twenty spinal procedures, and my fingers were reattached. A lot of physical therapy was required to get me to walk, and there was no mobility in my neck and shoulders. Pain ran rivers throughout my entire body, from my shoulders down to my sewn fingers, from the top of my head to my sacrum and all the way down the left side of

---

I decided to risk living with severe physical pain, because I knew that if I had my mind back, I could start to make myself heal.

---

my body. For quite a long time, I couldn't move at all. My daily routine was lying flat on my back, staring out a tiny window at a patch of blue sky and a hint of waving palm tree. I tried to hold images in my mind of what life had been like when I'd been able to move, dress myself, go to the bathroom on my own, go to work. Pain medication fogged my mind.

It was a challenging time, to say the least. Finally, I realized that no matter how much physical pain I was in, the medication caused me a greater pain: that of losing full mind function. It was painful to feel disconnected, to feel stupid and unable to communicate.

I decided to risk living with severe physical pain, because I knew that if I had my mind back, I could start to make myself heal. So I did it. And I moved through it, one second at a time, one minute at a time, by using the formula. It began with the simple but agonizing task of learning to breathe again; each breath caused pain, and I saw that my entire system was in a clinch. I literally said to myself: "Okay. Take a breath." I'd take a breath, and then acknowledge the achievement: "Great. You did that and it worked. Now take another one." After a while, I was breathing. I was accessing the life source again.

Living with so much pain, I went through a period of denial of my own ability to choose, a sort of "woe is me" phase. But soon I saw that I had to make a choice: I had to *see* myself choosing life. Then I had to go a step further and imagine that I could exist with *quality* of life. I had to say, out loud to myself and to my support system, "I'm going to do this. I'm going to make it."

My faith inspired me. Love inspired me. Determination propelled me. I was not going to let the doctors be right. My destiny was my choice. I chose life on my own terms. Again, it worked! I am still here. And I'm still dealing with pain, but I've learned many different ways to manage it. I've found wonderful, supportive doctors whose methods work with my own holistic ones.

My own search for healing led me to a new and fulfilling career as a practitioner of homeopathic healing arts, which I practiced for eleven years. My approach to vibrant health, whether through Reiki, chakra and crystal healing or meditation, has as its cornerstone the "see it, say it, make it so" formula.

Everyone can effect their own physical healing using this methodology. Again, this has proven to be true over and over in my own life. I'm an emotional eater; I've been so my whole life long, yo-

yoing and experimenting with weight-loss programs. I knew how to lose weight, but my eating habits made sure I never kept it off. Limited mobility from the accident compounded the issue and, in April of 2007, I weighed two hundred fifty five pounds. My doctor told me that he'd give me ninety days to get my blood sugar down to a normal level before taking aggressive action against potential diabetes.

Today, two years later, I've lost ninety-seven pounds (and counting). How? I envisioned myself healthy, with a normal blood sugar level. I called on the support of my friends, telling them my intention to get healthy and lose weight. I hired an organic chef to prepare healthy entrées so that being busy could

> *I used the formula to tackle one of my most tenacious self-limiting habits, and it has worked there, too!*

never be my excuse for engaging in old eating habits. Despite chronic pain, I began a light aerobic exercise routine. Now I can do fifteen minutes a day of movement that doctors once said I'd never manage at all. I used the formula to tackle one of my most tenacious self-limiting habits, and it has worked there, too!

It also worked when I was ready to reignite my passion for my former career. I'd thought that, after the accident and eleven years away from the corporate world, I could never reenter it. But after I wrote my book, and contacted former bosses and colleagues for testimonials, their glowing words reminded me of my natural abilities, my love for the work and the legitimacy of my experience and expertise. I saw myself creating a new company. As I'd chosen to in recovery from the accident, I thought, "I can do this!" And I did it. My new company, J-Team Database Marketing, Inc., fulfills a great need in the marketplace. Bringing all my experience, joy and will to bear, I am delightedly watching it take off.

See It, Say It, Make It So

Where others see obstacles, you can see opportunity. Verbalize your intention, take action, and you're on your way—to anywhere you want to go, any location or state of being. You can trust me on that one!

Julie Ann Cohn, winner of the Tempo and Echo Awards in advertising, brings over twenty-five years of leadership and innovative expertise to her new role as CEO of J-Team Database Marketing, Inc., ("ANALYZE, REALIZE AND ACTUALIZE:" visit www.J-TeamdDatabaseMarketing. com). She was founder of the Media Research Council, founder/Chairman/ CEO of Techmorrow Inc., and has worked for major ad agencies including DBB Worldwide, Western International Media and McCann Erickson on accounts such as Toyota, McDonald's, Disney, Pepsi, Ameriquest and American Airlines. She has been a regular guest speaker in such venues as the National Association of Database Marketing, The Advertising Research Foundation and the University of San Diego.

Julie, a Usui Reiki master, Magan David Life Energy master, doctor of metaphysics, Sufi Reiki master, shaman, crystal resonance therapist and minister, is also world-renowned for her teaching and healing work. She spent over eleven years as a transformational healer, teacher and empowerment coach; her CD, Transformational, *is available, as is her* Thank God I *story "Thank God I Died-The Third Time is The Charm" in the second of that series, written after her near-death experience. She is also founder and co-creator of The Blend™, and an active partner in Silver Unicorn Spirit Gifts. (See www.theempowermentstrategist.com and www.lightmindsthinkalight.com.)*

Julie's employees and clients all refer to her as their "best mentor." Her book, C.A.S.H.: Creating Achievement and Success Harmoniously, *seamlessly combines her business savvy and experience with her transformational teachings to bring awareness of the inextricable connection between the spiritual and the material, and between business achievement and personal achievement (www.JulieAnnCohn.com).*

Stand Up and Take Charge

Susan Elizabeth Santsche

I'll bet on two things about you, no matter your history or where you come from. The first is that life has presented you with at least one or two great challenges along the way; the other is that you have risen courageously, in your own way, to meet those challenges. Perhaps there was a time when you felt you'd lost everything. In less than ideal circumstances, it took great courage for you to stand up and take charge of your life. But you did it! And, in doing so, you became your own advocate. What if you could do the same when it comes to your health, and the health of your loved ones? I'm here to tell you that you can—and that really, you must. You have the power to save lives.

I've heard it said that an idealist is one who has gone through the fire—and thus been purified and inspired.

My ideals (of faith, passion, perseverance and resilience) have truly been tested. When my daughters were small, my husband was seriously injured and immobilized. Suddenly I became sole caregiver and provider for my family.

I also had a chance to turn adversity into opportunity, and to reframe a tragedy. Against all odds, I opened a business so I could provide for my family. For years I worked tirelessly in all my roles, raising my daughters and focusing on my husband's rehabilitation and recovery. Like so many busy women, I unconsciously relinquished responsibility for my own well-being.

My wake-up call came with an unexpected pregnancy when my daughters were nine and twelve. I'd been in survival mode for so long that, ironically, I'd risked my *own* survival; it had been years since I'd had a routine check-up. The doctors who discovered that I was pregnant also found that I had advanced cervical cancer. They decided the best course would be to perform a biopsy each month of my pregnancy to keep a close eye on the cancer. Then, after my son was born, I would have a hysterectomy.

This experience brought about deep changes in my thinking. I realized that, had I taken time to care for myself, too, I would not have been so compromised.

I saw that the unexpected gift of my son's life had possibly saved my own. I saw an opportunity to put my life into perspective, and asked myself: How do I want to live from now on? My coping mechanism was to give back. Realizing that a huge part of the purpose of my transformative experience was

---

What if you could become your own advocate when it comes to your health, and the health of your loved ones? I'm here to tell you that you can—and that really, you must. You have the power to save lives.

---

to share it with others and help them put themselves on the tops of their priority lists, I became even more proactive within my community, encouraging others to stay in tune with their bodies and become their own health care advocates.

Everything was going great; I was not expecting to be visited by yet another of life's challenges. But five years after my first bout with cancer, I was again diagnosed—this time with a very aggressive breast cancer. I'd been so encouraged by the changes I'd already made in my self-care. But now another important shift occurred. Re-framing once again, I really got it that it doesn't matter where you live, how big or how small; what matters is your intention and your commitment to greatness. To make a difference, *you* need to be the difference—overcoming life's challenges no matter what it takes.

And that's what I proceeded to do with my health. After the second diagnosis, my friend Meri said, "Okay. This time I want you to try putting together a binder with all your medical information in it." The binder, she explained, would give me

---

So I made the first step on what has become the path of an important mission: I stood up and took charge of my own health.

---

some control over what was happening, and keep all my records in one place. With all that information at my fingertips, I would truly be able to act as my own advocate. So I made the first step on what has become the path of an important mission: I stood up and took charge of my own health.

Meri had had direct experience with the vital need for access to medical information. Her sister Theresa, a schoolteacher with two small children, had been diagnosed with breast cancer. She'd gone through a mastectomy, radiation, chemotherapy and other treatments. We all thought she was in remission until a cough landed her in the hospital. For months, until she demanded a chest X-ray, every doctor she saw told her she had asthma or bronchitis. Her family, desperate for answers, gathered all of her medical records into a binder. Copies of X-rays, lists of medications, treatment schedules—the binder made Theresa a full participant in her care, and gave her and her family a timeline, a record and a sense of control in a frightening situation.

After these valiant efforts, though, Theresa passed away at the age of thirty-seven. Her story inspired me to take charge of my own health, and to create the Courage Awareness Movement, the Health Advocacy Binder and the online Health Concierge Advocacy Program to help others to stand up and become their own health care advocates.

I can't tell you how many people I've spoken with who have lost family members and friends because of missing or inadequate health information. With illness, time and knowledge are of paramount importance. When you're sick, scared and overwhelmed, it's impossible to remember your entire health history. You may not recall, for example, the name of a medication that caused heart problems before and that you do *not* want to take again! And, if you are too sick or stressed to act on your own behalf, loved ones will have access to all your records, too. That brings everyone more peace of mind, and might very well save lives.

The binder made a huge difference in my second experience with cancer. Every time I had a test, went to the doctor, started a medication or learned a bit of family health history, I asked for a copy or wrote down the information in my binder. I felt I had some control over the quality of my care, and better knowledge of my own body. It was also helpful to my doctors, saving huge amounts of time that might have been wasted— to my detriment—trying to gather records from multiple sources. Instead, I had all of them in one place.

The Courage Awareness Movement began with "Night of Courage," an annual event I created to celebrate the courage we all can feel proud of when we stand up and take charge of our own lives, no matter our circumstances or how "small" we feel in terms of our achievements. This was a bold move in such a rural community, where people might not feel empowered enough to believe that when they pursue their passion and vision, their path will appear. But the event has grown every year. After all, whether it's overcoming an illness, enduring the loss of a loved one, or just the kids spilling the milk, it takes courage to live our lives.

Night of Courage quickly expanded to Courage Awareness, a movement to help people realize their true potential as human beings. Courage Awareness became the platform for helping others take charge by becoming their own health advocates, and the Health Advocacy Binder became an integral part of Courage Awareness. It includes everything you need to keep track of your health, including universal tips for self-care, emergency resources, speaking with health professionals and sharing information with your family.

When Theresa was alive, she took great pleasure in paying it forward by always covering the toll for the car behind her. Courage Awareness honors Theresa's memory by dedicating its work to her, including her story in the Binder, and paying it forward by using all proceeds from purchased Binders to provide Binders to those in need.

When Mark Victor Hansen and I spoke about the future of sustainable health care, he made a beautiful gesture over me and said, "I ordain you, Susan, to lead the charge."

The newest development in Courage Awareness was created after that inspiring moment: the Health Concierge Advocacy Program, an online version of the Binder that you, your family or anyone you choose can access from anywhere, at any time. All your records are stored in a secure e-vault handled by you, or by a

---

When Mark Victor Hansen and I spoke about the future of sustainable health care, he made a beautiful gesture over me and said, "I ordain you, Susan, to lead the charge."

Medical Coordinator if you need one. We carefully file our credit reports and financial statements; there's no reason why, in the digital age, we should not have control over our medical records too. Imagine the possibilities for us, and within our health care system, if we all were proactive about our own health!

The time is now, with health care reform so present in the collective consciousness, to join in creating the change we need to see in health care. It's like recycling; it begins at home. It begins with you. Stand up and take charge—become a part of the Courage Awareness Movement!

Susan Elizabeth Santsche believes in giving back and paying it forward. A beauty industry expert honored with one of only ten Global Salon Business Awards in the US, Susan has her own line of skin care products; created and owns The Spa and Salon at Personal Choice in Eureka, California, and is author of the forthcoming skin care book Faces *(the first in a series). Committed to being an inspiring voice for the "little guy" in small business and small-town America, Susan is a salon and spa industry educator and a business coach for OneCoach Company.*

A cancer survivor and health advocate, Susan created the Courage Awareness Movement, and, in 2005, "Night of Courage," an annual celebration of personal stories of courage. "Courage Under Fire," a one-day seminar for growth and fulfillment, is now a part of Courage Night events. It has inspired Master Mind Groups to support each other in personal growth as "accountability buddies." A Health Concierge Advocacy Program and a Health Advocacy Binder are the major projects of the Courage Awareness Program. Bring the Courage Awareness Movement to your hometown. Visit www.CourageAwareness. com and www.CourageNight.com. To learn more about Susan visit www. SusanElizabeth.com and www.MySpace.com/AuthorSusanElizabeth.

The Audacity of Selfless Giving

Ken Ng

C hinatown, like any neighborhood in New York City, is full of
stories. Stories that surprise you, shock you, and shape you.
My family has many exciting, colorful, funny and heartwarming
stories. It is through one story in particular that I discovered
their most valuable legacy.

It was 1939. The Japanese had been bombing Canton, China,
for two years before they finally occupied my mother's village,
seizing my Grandfather's herbal medicine practice, home and
property. Broken by the loss, and the violence of the occupation,
he died soon after.

Mama was still just a teenager, but she was already performing
under the guidance of a renowned master of the classical Chinese
opera. She was away when her family was forced to join the
masses of people on the run from the Japanese.

As was the custom with people from the upper class, my
grandmother, Popo, had bound feet. She couldn't run; in fact, she
could barely walk.

"I will carry you," my aunt said to her mother, knowing
full well it could be days, weeks, or months before they found
a permanent safe place, before she would be able to rest. With
the soldiers closing in, my aunt hoisted her mother on her back
and carried her to a safe house, hiding her on top of a straw roof

until the soldiers had gone. That was the beginning of their long, arduous journey through the Canton countryside.

Thinking only of her mother's safety, my aunt piggybacked her from village to village, from relative to friend, and from friend to acquaintance. When they ran out of acquaintances they stayed in sheds, in barns, in abandoned buildings. For almost two years they hid from the Japanese, homeless, hungry, lost.

One day my aunt was captured while searching for food. Concerned for the safety of her mother, she fought to survive, enduring daily attempts by her captors to beat and humiliate her into providing information.

"I will carry you," my aunt said to her mother, knowing full well it could be days, weeks, or months before they found a permanent safe place, before she would be able to rest.

During this time Mama made her way to Hong Kong, where she performed in the opera—and worried about her family. She had lost track of her parents and sister after the occupation, and feared she would never see them again.

Meanwhile, the Japanese realized my aunt had no useful information. This made it easier for her to escape. Miraculously, she found Popo, safe with relatives.

"Leave me here," Popo instructed her daughter. "Go find your little sister and take care of her."

Knowing her sister had settled in Hong Kong, my aunt made her way to the city and found Mama. She told her the sad news of their father's passing, and that she had carried Popo on her back to keep her alive. She told other stories too, stories of the countless relatives, friends and strangers who helped hide them from soldiers, feed them, keep them safe. In Hong Kong my aunt dedicated her life to caring for Mama, becoming her handmaiden, protector and confidante.

It wasn't long before Mama boarded the Coolidge steam ship with dozens of fellow actors bound for America. She soon found success, starring in leading roles in Chinese opera venues, earning the admiration of audiences, maestros and men (including, eventually, my father). Ever grateful to her heroic sister, Mama helped her and Popo open a restaurant in Canton after the war, sending money to help support them and other relatives.

My grandmother died within a few years. She was not killed or tortured by the Japanese. She did not die of starvation. My aunt's supreme act of courage and dedication ensured their safety.

But the story doesn't end there.

In the United States Mama became a diva of classical Chinese opera, famous in San Francisco and New York. She traveled, she performed and somewhere in the midst of all that managed to have children.

My aunt's supreme act of courage and dedication ensured their safety.

Of Mama's many admirers, perhaps the most notable was a wealthy businessman from New York who owned half of Chinatown. One day he showed up at her apartment in San Francisco. Recently widowed, he was traveling to Hong Kong in search of a new bride to take care of him, and he had come to say hello on his layover.

"You must be very careful choosing a bride," Mama told him. "If you choose a pretty young wife, she may run around on you. If you choose a bride that is too smart, she may cause trouble with your family." Mama handed him a piece of paper with a name and address. "Promise me you will go see this woman last," she urged, and he grudgingly agreed.

It was my aunt's name on that piece of paper. The businessman kept his promise to Mama. After he met my aunt, there was no need to search further; a few months later, they were married.

Mama knew that my aunt, who was twenty-eight at the time of her marriage, would not find a husband by the usual avenues. She was too old; the hardships of war had stolen her beauty. She was damaged, used, washed up. And she was illiterate. When she entered the United States she could only sign an "X" for her name. Mama saw her chance to pay it forward by helping her sister live a life of peace and privilege.

> *I believe that women are the force and the leaders for a positive, constructive change on this earth. I believe that women will lead us to peace, and I am totally committed to accelerating that growth.*

My aunt would become a hugely successful entrepreneur in her own right, parlaying funds from her husband's gifts into smart investments. She also helped raise me, and my siblings. We called her Yeemah, which means *second mother.*

It is the legacy Mama and Yeemah created that drives me today, their audacity of selfless giving. And it is that very attribute that brought them both much good fortune and happiness.

I believe that women are the force and the leaders for a positive, constructive change on this earth. I believe that women will lead us to peace, and I am totally committed to accelerating that growth. Women have always been my mentors, friends and confidantes. It began with my Mama and my Yeemah, two shining examples of an unbending will to succeed, to defy the odds and to not just survive, but thrive.

Today, I pay it forward, helping women break through the glass ceiling. Helping women feel whole and worthy. Helping women get in touch with their passion and make the choice to go for it. Helping women discover and practice self-care, take control of their lives and make the changes necessary to live the lives they have been longing for.

Yes, Chinatown is full of stories, but the best stories are those of ordinary people helping others in extraordinary ways. Thank you, Mama. Thank you, Yeemah.

After thirty years in comprehensive wealth management, Ken Ng pursued his passion to serve senior citizens and empower women, launching Hawaii Performance Magazine. He is a principal at LifeQuest Hawaii, where he helps individuals and organizations become navigators and champions of change by serving as a consultant and certified life coach. Inspired by his mother and aunt, Ken recently launched "Diva To Be," a coaching program for women in search of power, passion and authenticity.

Don't Wait for a Wake-Up Call

Howard Kay

How does a so-called health and wellness "expert" launch a book from a coronary care unit? I'm here to tell you. And that's the point—*I am here*.

One morning, just a few weeks before finishing my first book, I felt a little dizzy. I lay down to rest. Then I felt *a lot* dizzier. When I started to feel pain in my chest, I realized something was very seriously wrong. Although I preferred natural treatments for illness whenever possible, I decided I had better go to the emergency room to have it checked out.

As I was being driven to the hospital, I thought, "Boy, this isn't going to be good for the book!"

If I hadn't been in so much pain, I might have laughed at the irony of the situation. Thirty years of intense, passionate study in achieving optimal health, a total devotion to practicing what I preached and here I was maybe—probably—having a heart attack. Heck, I hadn't even eaten one morsel of red meat in over thirty years. How could this be happening to *me*, of all people?

"The book's not even finished yet. This is definitely *not* good" I thought. My mind was racing with "what-ifs." Would readers take my advice seriously if they knew? How was I going to explain this to my clients, much less my publisher? If I survived, how could I finish the book, much less dare to publish it?

Turns out, I was having a massive heart attack. And it was not my first near-death experience. The first time I almost killed myself, I nearly drove off a cliff.

Sixteen years ago, I fell asleep at the wheel. One morning, during my commute from my home in Encino to my office in Beverly Hills, I woke up just as my car tumbled out of control. Hurtling through the canyons during rush hour traffic, it's a miracle I didn't die—or harm anyone else.

I'm a fairly intelligent, analytical male, so falling asleep at the wheel made absolutely no sense to me. Despite having a very successful CPA practice, I rarely burned the midnight oil—even

If I survived, how could I finish the book, much less dare to publish it?

during tax season! Truthfully, I hated being a CPA. Despised it. I sure wasn't going to lose any sleep over it.

The night before my accident—and every night prior for years and years—I had enjoyed a solid eight hours of sleep and woke up feeling refreshed and ready for the day. Wellness was my passion. I ate well, exercised and led a very healthy lifestyle. Falling into a heavy sleep just hours after I woke up really came out of left field. It seemed totally illogical. So I did what seemed logical to me—I ignored it.

But then, shortly after the driving incident, I fell asleep again—while interviewing a client in my office. Then it happened again, and again, until finally I went to a sleep clinic to figure out what was going on. After hooking me up to machines and observing my sleeping patterns through the night, doctors determined that I had Restless Leg Syndrome (RLS).

With RLS my legs were kicking all night long. It was at the subconscious level, so I was never aware that it was happening. As a result, I never got the complete, deep sleep my body needed. My leg-kicking never woke me fully, but it kept me from REM sleep. So even though I felt awake and thought I was getting "good" sleep, my body was always exhausted.

The doctors gave me a choice: take a muscle-relaxing drug to stop the kicking, or keep falling asleep at inconvenient times. Since losing clients or crashing my car were not viable options, I took the drugs. Luckily, I experienced no side effects.

With the RLS in check, I went back to ignoring the issue. Because I no longer fell asleep during the day, I denied the fact that I had a problem. I told myself, and anyone who asked, "I sleep fine."

One day, nearly five years after the accident, a friend of mine asked me to test some products he was considering as a business opportunity: a magnetic sleep system, an infrared comforter and a pillow. As a relatively new friend, he had no idea I had RLS and had been on drugs for five years. After all, I didn't think I had a problem. Why would I tell anyone *else* that I had a problem?

Firmly believing the products had nothing to do with me, and fully believing magnetic and infrared energies would have zero

---

Falling into a heavy sleep just hours after I woke up really came out of left field. It seemed totally illogical. So I did what seemed logical to me — I ignored it.

---

effect on my sleep, I agreed to test them out. I put the system on my bed, took my RLS meds and went to sleep.

The next morning two things happened that got my attention: I popped out of bed like toast from a toaster, and I remembered my dreams. I never felt so energized. And I remembered my dreams! For twenty years I assumed I didn't dream at all—and yet, on this morning, I could recount multiple dreams in vivid detail.

Within two weeks I had weaned myself from my RLS meds and was sleeping fine—no RLS. After three weeks of using the magnetic sleep system, I had a realization: my acid reflux was gone! For years I had experienced severe heartburn several times a week, like clockwork.

It was then that I realized I had been in denial with a capital "D." The meds hadn't solved the problem; the pills just stopped the symptoms from manifesting. I still had RLS symptoms. Or at least I *had* RLS for nearly five years—and probably longer, undiagnosed—until I tested out the magnetic sleep system.

"No more meds and three weeks without acid reflux is a pretty dramatic change," I thought. "I've got to find out what this is all about."

I set out to learn everything I could about magnetic and far-infrared energies: why our bodies need them, why we don't have enough of them in modern society and how we can access these necessary energies to achieve optimal health.

I had studied the human body, nutrition and wellness for years, but never with this much passion and intensity. I was a man on a mission. It became clear that I had found my true calling. Within one year, I sold my accounting practice and started a coaching practice to share the wealth of information I had learned.

In my studies, personal experience and professional wellness coaching practice, I had discovered the seven essentials for lifelong health and wellness: oxygen, water, sleep, nutrition, pH balance, movement and magnetic energy. And I knew firsthand that most people have no idea they need all of these elements— much less the proper way to get them—in order to return to pure health (their natural state).

So, after ten years on my true path, I decided to write a book to share my knowledge with the world. I found a publisher and dedicated myself to creating the best, most informative book on wellness available. Just as I made it to the homestretch, it happened.

Out of nowhere, I had a massive heart attack.

"It's a good thing you came in," one of the ER doctors said. "Another couple of hours, and you would have died."

"But I'm so healthy," I thought. I walked the talk, making sure I got proper nutrition, exercise and all seven essentials for optimal health. A heart attack? Me? It all seemed so—illogical.

Another doctor asked, "Do you have a history of high cholesterol? Any heart disease in your family, Mr. Kay?"

"Well, yes." I answered begrudgingly. I felt sunk, as if all my hard work on the book would be wasted.

And then it hit me. My body was trying to tell me something. I had high cholesterol in my youth, but because I dedicated my life to health and wellness, I never bothered to get it checked later on. I thought I had solved the problem—forgetting that, just because symptoms dissipate, the illness has not necessarily disappeared.

The doctors explained that one of my major arteries was one-hundred-percent blocked. With my family history of heart disease, I should have been on top of it with regular stress tests and cholesterol monitoring. The heart attack was not an event

In that moment in the ER - hooked up to machines, lucky to be alive—I realized that knowledge may be power, but it's useless if we don't act on it.

that started and finished that morning. It was the culmination of years of denial. I knew the information was available to me, but I chose to ignore it. In that moment in the ER - hooked up to machines, lucky to be alive—I realized that knowledge may be power, but it's useless if we don't act on it.

Will Rogers said, "We're all ignorant, just on different topics." Just as I chose to be ignorant about my RLS eleven years ago, I chose to be ignorant about genetic preconditions to heart disease, believing my healthy lifestyle made it a moot point. As it turns out, though my lifelong commitment to health could not prevent the heart attack, my lifestyle had ultimately saved me from a *fatal* heart attack.

On my second day in the hospital, I realized that my heart attack could be a powerful tool in getting my message across. Rather than derailing the book, my coronary wake-up call helped me illustrate the point that most health and wellness opportunities arrive without a drum roll—with no recognizable warning.

September 7 I was admitted to the hospital with a stroke. The blood vessels in my brain became inflamed and burst. A stroke is the next step higher than a heart attack and it is a sign that my blood pressure was too high. This was another indication that I was ignorant of the principles of good health that I was teaching. I ignored one of the basics, and that was that blood pressure, cholesterol and heart rate need to be monitored by a primary care physician.

Yet, if we pay attention to our health *before* the car crashes, strokes and heart attacks, we can achieve optimal health. We can save our own lives before we even know they need to be saved.

Howard Kay is the author of You Were Born Healthy, Choose to Stay That Way: The 7 Essentials to Lifelong Health & Wellness *(www. YouWereBornHealthyBook.com). After selling his successful Beverly Hills public accounting and tax practice after twenty five years as a CPA, Kay answered his true calling and began his career as an international wellness coach and consultant ten years ago. Building on more than thirty years of intense, devout study of optimal health, Kay teaches people how to make their bodies work more effectively, and avoid breakdowns using natural means whenever possible. He is currently working on his second book,* How to Avoid Jet Lag.

Financial Freedom for All

Jim Griffin

D id you know that that most disabled people cannot get life insurance to protect their families? Or home or auto insurance, or supplemental insurance should they get injured at work? That's right, work. Did you know a great number of disabled people do work, and many for substantial salaries? Well, I didn't know any of this myself, until about three years ago when I got a phone call that changed my life.

That fateful call came from an old friend of mine, Mark Victor Hansen. On the line with him was Tom Sullivan, a sixty-five-year-old man who was born blind and still went on to graduate from Harvard and become a leader in the disabled community. He is also a playwright, a singer and even an athlete.

"Jim," Mark said, "You've done all of these insurance products for Wall Street banks." Tom added, "But there's absolutely nothing available for people in the disabled community as far as insurance." This surprised me. I'd always assumed the government took full care of disabled people. Then Mark and Tom gave me their pitch: Did I think I could create insurance products specific to the disabled community? "Sure," I said. I hung up the phone, having no idea what I'd gotten myself into.

I was in my early sixties, and I'd started in the insurance business when I was twenty-seven. I kicked off my career with a real stroke of luck: I insured Elvis Presley's and Colonel Tom Parker's interests in all of Elvis's movies. From there I went on to work mostly on Wall Street, insuring hedge funds and big firms.

I knew from my experience that any disabled person, to get insurance, would have to take a physical—and would inevitably fail it. So I knew that whatever plan I came up with would have to be from scratch. I was an innovator in the insurance business. I created the first variable insurance products to fund corporate

> I knew from my experience that any disabled person, to get insurance, would have to take a physical—and would inevitably fail it. So I knew that whatever plan I came up with would have to be from scratch.

liabilities, and products to help executives further their bonuses. I've also always loved a good challenge. But not until I plunged into this challenge did it really hit me: by creating insurance products for disabled people, I was trying to do something no one else had ever done, maybe never even tried.

I needed to study up on the world of the disabled, so I went to Washington, D.C., and spent much of the next year there engulfed in an astonishing learning process. I was amazed by the number of associations dedicated to lobbying for the disabled. I had no idea how organized and effective the disabled community was, even though these associations had to raise all of their own money (something else I didn't know).

But going into this work, the single greatest revelation I had was that many disabled people were already out in the workforce. I didn't know that people who were so disabled were out making forty or fifty or sixty thousand dollars a year. I didn't know that there was already a movement in place whereby people who are disabled were able to get jobs.

Much of this movement is possible because of the passage of the Americans with Disabilities Act of 1992. Thirty years ago, if you were born with a severe disability, you were likely put into an institution. But no longer. In fact, I have someone working for me who has a great brain—and extreme cerebral palsy. He graduated from the University of Maryland and went on to graduate school at Catholic University. Even twenty years ago, his story may not have been possible.

I realized I wasn't starting a movement so much as I was joining one. I also realized that it wasn't about insurance. It was about helping disabled people obtain complete financial freedom. Financial freedom begins with getting a job. You become financially free when you have good insurance coverage for your family and good investment opportunities. So, to help the disabled community achieve this freedom, I started the company 54 Freedom. The name of my company comes from the 2001 census. It showed that, at any given time, fifty-four million Americans are disabled. More than half have temporary disabilities from conditions such as short-term injuries; twenty-six million people are permanently disabled. That's one out of every eleven people.

The first step our company took was a baby step. I had been to Family Café, a convention in Orlando sponsored by numerous corporations that pay for four days at Disney World for families with disabled parents or children. While there, I learned that many working disabled parents use all of their disposable income to purchase extra care and equipment. As a result, they have no money to buy any kind of insurance, so if they get hurt or die, their families will be devastated.

We teamed up with Lloyd's of London and created our first two policies—ten thousand-dollar death and dismemberment polices that cost thirty-five or fifty-four dollars per year. We offered this policy to that young man with cerebral palsy who works for us (although at the time he worked for someone else). The policy included a discount pharmacy card. It was the first time in his life he ever had insurance. It was a major step toward his own complete financial freedom, and he felt great about it.

We worked with Lloyd's of London to create more products. In fact, with Lloyd's, we created the first policy to protect an already-disabled person's income. There's no physical; the policyholder just has to be employed. If the policyholder has

> *Lloyd's of London thought the policy was unbelievably creative. Their representatives said it was the most unique thing the company has done since it started in 1688.*

some sort of accident and can't work, her money is protected. It's a group association product, and such a good policy that we have brokers and CPA associations wanting to buy it. Lloyd's of London thought the policy was unbelievably creative. Their representatives said it was the most unique thing the company has done since it started in 1688.

Let me illustrate how freeing that policy is. One day, I had breakfast with a leader in the disabled community who was born with cerebral palsy. He was in his sixties, lived in a wheelchair and always had a smile on his face. He ordered a pancake, and I asked him if I could butter it for him. He said, "Sure." Then I asked if he wanted syrup, and he said, "Just a little, because I don't want to risk spilling it on me."

That's the kind of small thing disabled people have to think about day after day. And that's just syrup. Can you imagine how much they must preoccupy themselves to avoid injury? And not just because of the inconvenience of an injury—difficult for anyone, and certainly magnified in their cases—but also because of the financial ruin any injury could possibly bring, all because they can't get insurance.

We've since created other insurance products—accidental death and dismemberment, auto and homeowner insurance. We made products never made before, and to do so we had to overcome terrible market conditions. When we first started, the markets were great, so brokers were lazy, and we had to battle that. Then markets crashed, causing chaos, and we had to contend with that. But we persevered and, as a result, did what had never been done before.

But insurance is just the beginning. My vision is for 54 Freedom to be the first total financial resource center for the disability community. So we've added another component: an idea Mark and Tom had for a series of financial primers, easy-to-read resource books that give a brief on various financial aspects of the life of a disabled person. We're going to launch a new primer every ninety days. The first covers some basic financial principles, and the following three discuss benefits, legal matters and accounting, respectively.

We also plan on taking our company public so that anyone who is disabled can buy stock in it and make money. It will be an opportunity for disabled people to invest in a company that is investing in them. Our clear vision is to make 54 Freedom one of

The entire experience is also an endless revelation. My own little private issues are insignificant compared to what I see disabled people experiencing on a daily basis.

the best companies in America, a company that helps an entire population know a financial freedom it never dreamed possible. It hasn't been easy, and every day is a bit of a dog fight. But the challenge has been exciting. And to wrangle and strangle and push and prod carriers to create products for disabled people— products that are so good that non-disabled people are buying them—is both rewarding and fun.

The entire experience is also an endless revelation. My own little private issues are insignificant compared to what I see disabled people experiencing on a daily basis. And yet, their attitudes continue to amaze me. Another leader in the disabled community is a lawyer who has no arms and legs and therefore has these metal appendages. Once, in a hotel washroom, one of his arms accidentally fell off, and he turned to the guy next to him and said, "Could you give me hand?" When you feel a smiling, positive energy coming from someone who can't get out of a wheelchair, or who is blind, it's amazing.

There's a financial freedom movement in the disability community. They are working; they're not going to be institutionalized and they're a force. I am honored, and humbled, to be a small part of that great force.

Jim Griffin is the CEO and founder of MoneyIns and 54 Freedom. He spent twelve years as a general agent for Massachusetts Mutual Life Insurance Company in New York, leading one of the largest agencies in the country. Jim was a consistent winner of the insurance industry's Master Agency Award, and one of twenty-five general agents chosen in 1990 for the leadership pilot program of the American College in Bryn Mawr, Pennsylvania. He founded his firm in 1994. His many corporate clients include Morgan Stanley, First Boston, Shearson, Lehman Brothers, Wasserstein Perrella and Tiger Management.

In 2006, Jim founded 54 Freedom to create a one-stop financial resource for people with disabilities. He co-authored Chicken Soup for the Soul: A Financial Primer for the Disability Community, *the first in a series of financial empowerment books for people living with disabilities. To learn more about Jim, visit www.54Freedom.com.*

Learn to Fly Solo

Nicholas R. De Stefano

I discovered, from within, that I could be the person I choose to be. However, in order to accomplish that, I had to have complete faith and trust in myself, my instincts, my thoughts, my objectives and—most of all— the fact that I had the courage to make it all happen.

I also realized that, even when others want to help you, they cannot know your innermost desires. They are very subjective with their offers of assistance, and oftentimes their advice has no bearing on your intended outcome. Sometimes, a friend's advice can be quite good. But if you rely upon the help of others to move forward, and that help doesn't come, you can't move forward. The best guarantee of moving forward is learning to fly solo.

Once you learn to fly solo, you can truly pursue your dreams without any inhibitions. There will still be obstacles. In everything we do, there are always obstacles. But achieving your dreams isn't about encountering obstacles; it's about overcoming them.

In my work with others, I have found that one of the main elements holding people back from pursuing their dreams, their hopes and their wants is that they haven't clearly defined their goals. They don't even know what it is they want. And the reason they don't know what they want is that they don't really know who they *are*. More specifically, they haven't realized their special value in this world.

You have value. No one in this world can do what you do. To admit that is neither bragging nor a put down of others; it's just a simple statement of fact. Others may, and can, do something similar to what you do, but no one else is you. I learned what my value was during a crucial period seventeen years ago. Until then, I had always been independent, always relied mostly on myself, and that was true for as long as I could remember.

> *You have value. No one in this world can do what you do. To admit that is neither bragging nor a put down of others; it's just a simple statement of fact. Others may, and can, do something similar to what you do, but no one else is you.*

According to my parents, when I was two, my mother would put me in a harness and tie me to the fence. It was a common practice back then that made it easier for parents to keep an eye on their children. Problem was, I always managed to find a way out of the harness.

When I was ten years old, I started my own neighborhood bicycle repair business as well as a shoe-shining business. Soon after, I worked at a local gas station part-time; and I picked up other various jobs over my school years. Eventually, I dropped out of high school and joined the army. I wanted to go to Japan—but instead I was stationed in France, where I finished the requirements for my GED and met my wife.

So I was always independent. But it was seventeen years ago, when I was diagnosed with prostate cancer, that I fully realized that about myself. I underwent a radical prostatectomy, and the recovery took almost two years. As if that wasn't enough, I was also going through a divorce. My wife at the time stayed with me for a year, until the worst of the cancer and recovery were over, before we finally separated. But during those two years, I went through a grueling process of self-discovery. I found it necessary to question my very existence and being. I questioned survival itself, and its importance in our world. I asked myself an array of questions to get at the essence of who I am. I looked into past experiences, going back as far as I could, and whenever I started to feel uncomfortable, I knew I was hitting on something I needed to fully examine.

I bore to my essence, and understood why I was so independent. I learned why so many other people are not independent. And I also learned that my unique value to this world could be in helping others become more independent themselves. To help others become independent, the first thing I did was write a book, *Who Sleeps in Your Skin?* The book is all about teaching others to be steadfast in their convictions while focusing on the positives in their lives, so that they can be more independent

---

I bore to my essence, and understood why I was so independent. I learned why so many other people are not independent. And I also learned that my unique value to this world could be in helping others become more independent themselves.

---

and achieve their goals. Ultimately, it's about knowing yourself, understanding yourself, liking *and* disliking yourself, all so you can live a life without limitations.

The first element to pursuing your dreams lies in knowing what they are. This requires knowing who *you* are, your value. But this is where many people run into the second element that prevents them from achieving their dreams: they lack the confidence and courage to pursue them.

There's so much in each of us that's not really us, but rather the usually negative, oftentimes well-intentioned influence of others. Most of it stems from childhood. Without realizing it, we often instill fear, guilt, confusion, uncertainty and dependence in our children by overcorrecting, misjudging, overstating and disallowing creative exploration. This haunts us as children, and it haunts us later in life. Whenever I ask a client what's holding him back, it's usually something that happened to him when he was a child, something he was scolded for or made to feel guilty about. But when that client can examine the past incident through the lens of the present, he can break free from its negative power.

Understanding the problem is just the beginning. Much of the real work toward building a more confident, more independent self comes after the understanding. And that is a lifelong process that involves the use of various survival power tools, like commitment, self-discipline and—most of all—courage.

After I got out of the army, I launched into an almost indescribable series of jobs—fourteen of them over twelve years. I did everything from sales for Fuller Brushes to staff management at Prudential. Along the way, I also got my college degree in three years at Bryant University. Successful as I was in my work, though, I just didn't like what I was doing. I was too independent to be subordinate to others.

So I decided to start my own business. It was a risky decision. My life was in a shambles at the time. I was in the midst of a divorce, and I faced a future of uncertainty with no money and a large amount of debt. But I didn't focus on the negatives. I focused on the positives of what I was about to do, and the strongest positive I had was my confidence in myself. No matter what you're trying to accomplish, you do have positives that you can focus on that will help you achieve your dreams.

Another key tool in the process of change is learning to recognize the wisdom of others. I was in international costume jewelry, and while I encountered many hardships over my twenty-seven years in the business, I also reaped many rewards, not all of them financial. I got to travel all over the world and share experiences with people of many different cultures. I learned that all of us share the common bonds of love and compassion. I learned that we all share the same values in life and family, and I learned that regardless of our cultural differences, we really are one. I also learned to appreciate each human being for exactly who that person is. I learned how to acknowledge that person's value and contributions to mankind.

Flying solo includes change. People tend to fear change because they fear being removed from their comfort zone. But change is a challenge to learn new things, an opportunity to be creative and get involved in something different. Change is

> *Before you can create your future, you must live in the present. And before you live in the present, you must edit your past, examining all those things that prevent you from moving forward.*

good, positive, stimulating and necessary for our well-being, so in actuality, we shouldn't fear change. Rather, what we ought to fear is *not* changing.

The entire process also involves failures. In fact, our entire lives involve failures, but I've never liked the word "failures." I prefer to call them learning experiences. Without making errors, how can we learn? Failure is an idea that, when applied to humans, means the opposite of success. So failure is interpreted as a negative, usually as applied to a specific goal. But to say someone failed is to assume you know that person's ultimate destiny. For instance, I was let go from many jobs, and that would suggest that I failed. But because I was let go from those jobs, I eventually started my own business, which afforded me many forms of success—financial, mental, emotional and cultural.

The point is that we are always on our path, even when it feels like we're not. We each have an origin and a destiny, and for the longest time we may not know what that destiny is. In order to cope with and survive my recovery from cancer, I adopted the idea of examining my life, something Socrates told us long ago we needed to do. As a result, I ended up with this entire new life of helping others shape their own futures. Before you can create your future, you must live in the present. And before you live in the present, you must edit your past, examining all those things that prevent you from moving forward.

My new life, my new direction, didn't happen all at once. It was over time that I came to appreciate my skills, my creativity and my keen understanding of the behavior of others. And I honed my ability to communicate. I learned to be skillful and kind—and hard or soft, depending on what was called for. In most major ways, I'm really no different from anybody else. I'm able to help people in a unique way; that's my gift, and I use it every day. Anytime I can help someone, I do. And usually my help leads people to realize what their gift is, and how they can use it to benefit us all.

Nicholas R. De Stefano has a BSBA from Bryant University with a major in management and a minor in economics. He has over forty-four years of experience in marketing and sales, and for twenty-seven years he owned a very successful international jewelry distribution business. Currently living in Florida, Nick is a licensed real estate broker with experience in commercial sales, marketing and business brokerage. He is also a business coach and consultant specializing in helping others overcome personal obstacles so that they can achieve the careers and lives they dream of. Nick's book, Who Sleeps In Your Skin? *and more information about his work are available at www.wsiys.com.*

How Elevators Changed My Life

Ron Edgar

E arly in my corporate life, I learned that the most effective way to deliver a message or teach people how to sell and endorse my product was to put on seminars and training sessions. In these sessions, I helped others create their sales persona by showing them how to share their enthusiasm. The better I got at the sessions, the more I was asked to do, and eventually I was speaking to audiences of up to three hundred people.

But there was a problem. Every time I had to speak in front of a group of more than five people, I got physically ill before and after the seminar. Truth be told, I actually got a nasty case of butterflies even when I was called upon to speak at a meeting. Once I was in front of the crowd, I was fine—not sweating bullets or anything. It was just before and after that I was a mess.

I started to get angry at myself over this problem. I knew that if I kept on like this I would eventually be unable to deliver the information I needed to deliver. I'd also noticed that, though I could push myself through every speech, I would gracefully bow out of speaking engagements when given the opportunity to do so. I knew I had to find a way to overcome this problem. My business, and my sanity, depended on it.

You can talk yourself into anything if you are seriously determined to overcome an obstacle. It may take grit, perseverance and a few boxes of tissue, but you can overcome anything. One day, while headed to a conference where I would be doing most of the training, my butterflies doing a circus act, I passed a co-worker who was talking about perfecting his elevator pitch. Being in sales, I knew quite well how to create a good thirty-second pitch; I'd even trained hundreds of people to do it. But when I heard the words "elevator pitch" this time, something clicked.

I immediately had what I thought then might be the dumbest idea ever: a way that I could force myself out of the physical reaction I had to public speaking. I would deliver my elevator pitch to as many people as I could, forcing myself to engage them, and I would do this several times a day. Where would I find these captive audiences? Why, in elevators, of course!

Elevators are everywhere and hard to avoid. I decided that, when I got on my office building's elevator, I would break with propriety and turn and face the crowd instead of facing the doors and reading numbers as we descended. I would have to talk to these people, and they would have no choice but to listen. So I stood in front of the elevator, waiting, listening to that telltale

---

You can talk yourself into anything if you are seriously determined to overcome an obstacle. It may take grit, perseverance and a few boxes of tissue, but you can overcome anything.

"bing" get louder the closer the car got. Finally it arrived, and the doors opened, but I was over in the bathroom losing my lunch. As I walked back to the elevator, the butterflies attacked again with an unprecedented vengeance. I was ready to beat a hasty retreat to the bathroom when I heard a voice say, "I'm holding the elevator for you."

To this day, I don't know which of the five unsuspecting souls who were on that initial elevator ride yelled out to me, but I'm still pretty sure he regretted it. That first time, I didn't begin with a boisterous, friendly, "Hi, my name is Ron, and I will be your host for this trip." Not even close. That first time, I started very timidly with a quiet, "Hey." But I started, and I finished, and I pulled it off.

When you make up your mind to tackle a challenge, the critical fact to remember is that the only person who can stand in your way is you. Also, once you decide to overcome a challenge, you'll notice there are two types of people—those who support you and

---

When you make up your mind to tackle a challenge, the critical fact to remember is that the only person who can stand in your way is you.

---

those who undermine you. The one undermining you can be a total stranger or a close relative. Whoever it may be, you need to thank him for his concern and tell him to get the hell out of the way. These people don't want you to change because it makes them look bad for not changing themselves.

And I did change. Slowly. I told no one what I was doing, but I did start to get regular encouragement, usually from a nice grandmotherly type who would smile and nod. Not everyone was supportive, of course, and who could blame them? Still, I learned quickly to negate the critics and absorb the positive feedback. And I started seizing every opportunity I could to ride the elevator. And not just in my building, for we had only ten floors. I often spent my lunch hour touring downtown Vancouver in search of taller buildings. Gradually increasing the height of the buildings I chose naturally increased the size of my audiences, and the process became easier. I'd ride to the top, scope out the facilities, wait for a good crowd of victims, then get on and banter my way to the bottom.

Forced to be spontaneous, I honed my technique through trial and error. For instance, I found that a humorous introduction with a call and response created a more receptive audience than jumping right in. My pitches were getting pretty entertaining, and often the crowd would be laughing by the time we reached the lobby. When you take a few moments to relax your audience and get to know them a little, you get a better result. Even when you have only thirty seconds, you need to resist the urge to rush right into your topic.

I started to get a regular following. I started to get groupies. I was having so much fun entertaining and enlightening the office tribes of Vancouver that it took almost two weeks before I noticed that I had stopped throwing up. Something that had ruled my world and caused me so much fear and anxiety had disappeared without any fanfare whatsoever. It had vanished—not with a bang, but a whimper.

There were a couple of other benefits, too. Often, by the time we got to the end of the elevator rides, people gave me their business cards. The elevator routines got me a few speaking engagements in the corporate world. And because each time I got on the elevator was like attending a spontaneity class, the process introduced me to a new style of training and has become a critical part of my

---

When you take a few moments to relax your audience and get to know them a little, you get a better result. Even when you have only thirty seconds, you need to resist the urge to rush right into your topic.

---

sales scripting. This determination to overcome my fears spilled over into everything else in my life. Roller coasters? Bring 'em on. Whitewater rafting? I'll get my paddle. Cliff jumping? Hold my towel! Get the crowd laughing at an event that's tanking? I'm your guy. The drive to overcome obstacles became so prevalent in my life that I later found out many of my colleagues were calling me "Fearless Ron." That cracked me up.

By overcoming my own fear, I was inspiring those around me, and they didn't even know what I'd gone through. They simply caught on to my enthusiasm and energy and wanted to be a part of it. Eventually, I began to tell the story of my growth and process. It had a huge impact on groups who watched me speak so comfortably in front of them, but it had even more impact on those who knew me well. They would have been the last to guess that Fearless Ron used to puke his guts out before meetings.

All of us have the capacity to change and overcome our obstacles. It's often just a matter of taking that first step to do it. And don't be depressed if your obstacle has you in despair. I personally had to reach a critical point, hit that low spot, before I could grow and move on. Oftentimes in such cases, those days that feel like the worst are, in retrospect, the ones that play out to be the best.

Known as "The Sales Pitbull," Ron Edgar has created innovative sales programs for a variety of sectors including telecommunications, transportation, retail and the public speaking circuit. He is also adept at helping others uncover or "create" their salesperson within. He has been privileged to consult with such icons as Mark Victor Hansen, Art Linkletter, Brian Tracy, Michael Gerber, Barbara Di Angelis and T. Harv Eker, to name a few. As a sales consultant and motivational speaker, Ron has brought his "no BS" sales approach to such companies as Best Buy, Staples, Microcell Telecom, Wal-Mart, Peak Potentials Training, M.V. Hansen & Associates and The JT Foxx Organization.

For more information on how to drive your sales organization to the next level, go to www.SalesPitBull.com.

Getting Noticed
Began with a Single Book

Joan Clout-Kruse

My current career came about because of the question, "How'd you do that?" Sometimes I was asking the question of others, and sometimes it was others asking the question of me—whoever was asking, that question has been integral to why I'm doing what I'm doing today.

My writing career began years ago in corporate America, where I held operational and management positions at various universities and Silicon Valley companies.

Ten years ago, I started my own business because of a single book that I wrote and published. This single book started my motivational speaking and training career. I had written my entire adult life, including many small books designed to help my readers achieve their goals and dreams. But I wanted this particular book to be as eye-catching as the other books in a bookstore.

I decided to write a book on Silicon Valley. There were already many books out there on the topic, but they were either about, or by, these mega-successful millionaires or billionaires who'd done something world-altering. I was interested in writing a book about *ordinary* Silicon Valley people, who had experienced different kinds of success—such as a woman who built and flew her own airplane while she was in her thirties.

A few years later, after publishing my book, I learned a key lesson—before you start writing your book, you should have a marketing plan. Marketing your book should be part of your plan for *writing* your book. There are many ways to market a book while you're writing it—or even before. For instance, you

> *A few years later, after publishing my book, I learned a key lesson—before you start writing your book, you should have a marketing plan. Marketing your book should be part of your plan for* writing *your book.*

can line up book reviews in various venues, print or on-line. You can send out a book proposal, and solicit testimonials. The best tip of all is to find a buddy or buddies who will motivate and support you while you are writing your book. Also, you can save lots of learning time by finding local authors and writing clubs who will give you tips and ideas on how to publish your book.

The actual writing of my book was a great growth period for me. I included the stories of fourteen ordinary Silicon Valley people, most new acquaintances and some who became good friends. And then those fourteen people actually helped me market the book, because they bought copies and passed them along to their clients and friends.

After that, I joked that I should have had thirty people in the book. I did hire a publishing consultant, and he came up with some great ideas. He got me on some book reviews, lined up signings at local book stores and even had the local NBC affiliate do a story on me and tied that into one local signing.

All in all, I sold about three thousand copies of my book. And that's not bad, since it came out in August 2001, one month before the tragic terrorist attacks on America.

Whenever I work with clients now, I find it crucial to establish realistic expectations right off the bat. Thirty thousand copies sold is awesome, and more than twenty thousand means you've got a best-seller. We identify a target market that will buy the book and then we set a realistic goal for the number of books we want to sell.

Even if you don't have a best-seller, your book gives you and your business an air of legitimacy. Your book becomes a marketing brochure that opens doors for you. Knowing you as a published author has a psychological effect on other people. It doesn't matter if your book is self-published or traditionally published, just so long as you are proud of the final product. It helps your self-esteem and confidence, and it elevates the confidence others have in you.

A published book is a new credential. Mine was. People began to see me as a celebrity author. They peppered me with questions—but never about my book. People were asking, instead, about the books *they* wanted to write.

Once people learned I'd written a book, they would literally ask me, "How'd you do that?" And I told them how I did that—so much so that I realized I was doing writing coaching for free. After a couple years of this free book-coaching, a friend of mine

---

Even if you don't have a best-seller, your book gives you and your business an air of legitimacy. Your book becomes a marketing brochure that opens doors for you.

---

asked me to attend a meeting for a new Chamber of Commerce he was starting in Silicon Valley. When introducing myself at the meeting, I stood up and said, as a joke, "Hi, I'm Joan, and I can help you write a book in ninety days or less." Five people approached me at the end of that meeting, and I realized I had a new career as a book coach.

It was about five years ago that I started this new business, and my speaking career. I began by helping people write books; then

I expanded to other fields—book proposals, articles, e-books, and "almost anything" writing. A couple of years later, I realized that my clients were having difficulty *selling* books. Granted, some of them didn't want to—they'd written personal little books that they wanted to give to just family and friends. Yet many wanted to sell lots of books, and wanted to know how to market them.

That's when I decided that I needed to add a marketing component to my business. This is the point at which I started asking others, "How'd you do that?" I certainly received some good ideas from the consultant who helped me market and promote my book. In addition, for the past five years I've spent hundreds and hundreds of hours learning about marketing, investing my time and money in books, classes and seminars.

I continue to be amazed by how much you can promote yourself on the Internet for so little money. Years ago, when I first started in business, it was all about direct marketing. Everything was so expensive, from buying ads in magazines

One of the most important lessons I've learned is that marketing is all about collaboration; you need the knowledge of other people if you're going to market successfully.

and newspapers to buying space in the phone book. One of the most important lessons I've learned is that marketing is all about collaboration; you need the knowledge of other people if you're going to market successfully. For instance, I have a major collaboration going with someone who is an expert on getting traffic to your website.

The marketing I've learned was put to the test with one of my major clients. This client is an amazing woman; she's a great, global public speaker, and she's created an educational comic book and a CD of rap and hip-hop songs that promote positive self-esteem. She hired me as a book coach.

The whole time we were compiling her book, I kept telling her she needed to begin marketing even before it was finished. She was so busy that she didn't develop a marketing plan at that time.

She didn't market after the book was finished, either. As I said, she's an amazing woman, but entrepreneurs with small businesses are really, really busy and rarely have enough time for extraneous tasks like marketing a book. So I decided to do some marketing for her.

The key to the success of your business and products is not that you market but HOW you market.

The first thing I did was have her change her website from a brochure website to a marketing website, one that was more focused on selling her products than on conveying information about her. I did all the copywriting for the new website and made it keyword-rich. I also wrote her a business plan, wrote proposals to get more business, worked on PR information, developed bios, wrote to her clients, set up newsletters and wrote blogs on her behalf.

The key to the success of your business and products is not that you market but HOW you market. The effort is paying off. In the four years before this new website existed, she never sold any of her products, and her earnings were based on her speaking engagements and training programs, which she got primarily through word-of-mouth advertising. She now is beginning to get more attention on her websites and is receiving more inquiries. Remember those hip-hop songs she wrote? They were picked up by a major music distributor, and her single will be released in a few months.

My own business is soaring, too—all because, ten years ago, I decided to write a book. A lot has evolved from that single book.

Part of the evolution resulted from my having specific expertise, such as my writing. But another, major part of the evolution has been the result of my simply asking others, "How did you do that?"

Along the entire journey, I've learned two sure things: the first is, never be afraid to ask how something is done. The second is, having learned how something is done, go and do it!

With more than three decades of writing, operational and management experience at Stanford University, UC Berkeley, Nikon Corporation and many other Silicon Valley companies, Joan Clout-Kruse has developed a keen sense of what it takes to get what you want through writing. As an entrepreneur who built her own successful writing and marketing consulting business, she empathetically helps business owners and professional speakers create books, e-books, articles and blogs and then develop low-cost marketing plans to find new customers and make more money.

Joan is the author and co-author of three books, and has hundreds of articles on the Internet covering writing, speaking, marketing and goal-setting. To learn more about Joan, visit www.Words4Money.com.

A Caregiver's Journey

Raquel C. Smith

M y whole life, I've always been a caregiver of some type or another. But it wasn't until I officially became a caregiver for my uncle that I stopped taking care of my most important patient: me.

It wasn't always that way. After I finished college, I moved to New York City to take care of my aunt who'd been diagnosed with lung cancer. But even though I was busy with that as well as with a job on Wall Street, I still took good care of myself. I knew I was taking good care of myself because I felt good. That sounds so simple, but people forget that if they're not feeling good, there's usually a reason.

Years later, I started suffering from severe headaches resulting from hypertension. Those headaches were what made me realize I was not taking care of myself. How come I was not taking care of myself? Well, the journey began in December 2005, when my uncle was diagnosed with an advanced prostate cancer. Overnight, I became a caregiver. It was a natural transition, partly because I just couldn't see myself not taking care of my uncle, and also because, of all family members, I was the one with the most flexible schedule and therefore most available.

Being my uncle's caregiver literally took over my life. Everything in my world stopped because my uncle was now the center of my world. My schedule had to revolve around his schedule so that I could take proper care of him. After a few months of being his caretaker, I started to get those headaches, and my blood pressure started to rise. I had no idea how I could have gotten so sloppy about my own health.

The bottom line is, caregivers usually put themselves last on the priority list—and that results in ill health for the caregivers. I did not give my own needs a second thought, because I wanted to make sure that my uncle was okay. I did not realize that if I was not taking care of myself, I would not be able to take care of him. How can you take care of someone else if you are not in good health yourself?

My uncle also knew I wasn't taking care of myself. There were times I would be sad, and he'd say, "You're not feeling well." I'd try to lie, but he knew the truth. Now, one of the first things I tell caregivers is that if you're faking a smile and falsely acting cheery,

---

Years later, I started suffering from severe headaches resulting from hypertension. Those headaches were what made me realize I was not taking care of myself.

---

your loved ones will know. Everything is energy, and we're giving off whatever energy we're feeling. If you're feeling low, the people you're caring for will feel low. Your health impacts their health, and may even make them feel worse.

One day, when I was in the room with my uncle, feeling lousy from another headache, the light bulb went on. I realized that other caregivers must be going through what I was going through, and that was the moment I decided I should start focusing on giving care to *caregivers*.

I found many support groups for caregivers, but most were inadequate. They met once a month or once a week for an hour, and since not all attending had time to share how they were really feeling, many went home feeling the same as when they'd arrived. Other support groups were good for what they were, but they focused on helping caregivers with day-to-day tasks. No one paid attention to the caregiver's emotional well being. No one instructed caregivers to make themselves the top priority on the caring list.

Statistics show that most caregivers die before those they're taking care of, because caregivers are not taking care of themselves. My feeling, then, was that before we worry about

---

Everything is energy, and we're giving off whatever energy we're feeling. If you're feeling low, the people you're caring for will feel low. Your health impacts their health, and may even make them feel worse.

---

daily tasks, we have to address self-care. So, shortly after my light bulb moment, I committed to taking better care of myself. And the first thing I did was take a step back to do some maintenance work on my spiritual condition.

In my coaching, the first thing I tell clients they need to do is to have a spiritual connection. By that I don't mean religion. I mean a connection with something greater than yourself— so that when you're feeling stressed, you can step back and reconnect with that force, and it can allow you to be at peace and go about caregiving with more ease. If my clients already have a spiritual connection, I urge them to maintain it. A spiritual connection can be anything—meditation once or twice a day for five or fifteen minutes. It can be a one or two-minute prayer. Just do something, because your alignment with a force greater than yourself will help with caregiving duties.

The next thing I did for myself was take some time away from my uncle, making arrangements for other family members to chip in and help take care of him. That time away gave me more time to build my business, so while I was taking care of myself, I was simultaneously setting up a system to help others take care of themselves, with my own experience informing how I would help others with *their* experience. In that time away, I was also rejuvenating myself.

Rejuvenation is absolutely essential to your mind, body and spirit; it is your refueling to keep going, your regular maintenance to keep your body in great health. We need to add gas to our cars, and we need to maintain them regularly to keep them running in top shape. Our bodies are no different. Some

> *Statistics show that most caregivers die before those they're taking care of, because caregivers are not taking care of themselves. My feeling, then, was that before we worry about daily tasks, we have to address self-care.*

things I do to rejuvenate are simple and cost little. At least once a week, I take a nice hot long bath. This soothes my nerves and gives me a renewed vigor to continue on my caregiving journey. I also like to sit quietly and be with me, just to quiet the mind and give it a chance to process stuff without outside influence. I love to walk along the beach, especially at sunset, and enjoy the beauty of creation. And my favorite thing is to get a massage, which relaxes my whole body and gets rid of any tension I'm holding.

A lot of caregivers feel guilty about leaving their loved ones, but I tell them that when they step away, they come back invigorated with positive energy and are better caregivers. This means that, ultimately, they're actually giving more time to their loved ones. I stress that caregiving is a joy, so when they feel frustrated or stressed out or burnt out, that all comes from not taking care of the self. If caregivers understand that, then they're more willing to remedy the problem, more open to taking a break.

I'm still caring for my uncle, but the experience is entirely different now because I'm taking better care of myself. I'm not going to say that I'm one hundred percent; everything is a work in progress. But I'm in the nineties. I'm now willing to ask for help from family members, I get my rest when I need it, and I'm honest about when I need rest. And I'm at peace with being a caregiver.

A spiritual connection can be anything—meditation once or twice a day for five or fifteen minutes. It can be a one or two-minute prayer. Just do something, because your alignment with a force greater than yourself will help with caregiving duties.

All caregivers need to be at peace with it if they are going to do it effectively. Many people have difficulty transitioning into being a caregiver, and I help them with that. They feel as if they're giving up their entire lives. But my life, my experience, can show them that they're not giving up their lives. They're still moving forward, they've just switched tracks.

It's an honorable job to be a caregiver. I've interviewed several people who said it was the best thing they could have done, and if they had to do it all over again, they would. We don't have much time on this earth. We need to spend the time we *do* have together lovingly, and not frustrate ourselves. I found a way to do that—which is why I feel so blessed, both professionally and personally.

Raquel C. Smith, MBA, MS, CMRC, is a caregiver coach and founder of the Caregiver Empowerment Summit, a life-changing, two-day event. She is also the CEO and founder of the Caregiver Coaching Institute, which certifies and trains effective caregiver coaches.

Raquel has combined her MBA in finance and MS in management information systems with her coaching training and experience to create a dynamic self-care-for-caregivers movement. This movement is changing the way caregivers provide self-care while caring for loved ones, and allows them to align their values with their goals and overcome challenges. Raquel has been a featured speaker at Conscious Life Expo, Los Angeles, and a contributor to several publications. She has also created several caregiver support products and has rightly earned the title of "Premier Caregiver Coach."

Raquel is the author of The Caregivers Guide to Self-Care *and* The Unexpected Journey: My Life as a Caregiver. *She is also the co-author of* Inspiration to Realization, Vols. II & III. *For more information on caregiver support, visit www.TheCaregiverOasis.com.*

Empower Consumers, Transform Communities

Bonnie Laslo

You should know right up front that I don't consider myself to be simply a real estate investor, even though I made millions investing in real estate. You should also know that I don't consider myself a landlord, even though I earn a living renting out houses and apartment buildings. And I am not a property manager, though part of my job is managing those properties.

I am a *Home Guardian*, working in cooperation with my tenants to improve their lives and transform their communities. A couple of years ago I took over a rental property in a low-income neighborhood. When I arrived to inspect the building, I noticed a roadblock, a swarm of law enforcement officers and even a news crew, interviewing the Mayor. I figured they were talking about the recent shooting in the area, but I wanted to know for certain what was happening. So I walked over and introduced myself.

"People are concerned about the shootings," the Mayor explained. "I'm here to shed light on the situation and try to solve the problem."

My partners and I decided to work with the city on finding a solution. When I took over the property, I knew that the area had some serious crime issues, and I was up for the task of turning it into a transitional area. Something had to give. Drug dealers and prostitutes owned the streets, and some of them even lived in my buildings. But I also knew that there were good people living behind these locked doors, and when they felt safe enough to come out, we could make it work.

A few days later I came back to the site with my team to make plans for renovation. When we arrived, the roadblock was still there. Law enforcement looked as though they had never left. The only difference in the scene, this time, was the absence of a news crew interviewing the Mayor. Over the course of a few months, my team and I completed improvements on the building and

---

But I also knew that there were good people living behind these locked doors, and when they felt safe enough to come out, we could make it work.

---

got the hard- core riffraff out of my good residents' neighboring homes. And still, every time we pulled up to the property we saw a roadblock, law enforcement and Kevlar vests as usual. It was getting to be a running joke.

"How can I help?" I asked the police. There was no question that we needed to speed up the process of this neighborhood's recovery. We spoke about what they were trying to do, and how I could help make it happen. For starters, I gave the police a key to the model apartment so they could use it for substation breaks, keep sodas in the fridge, monitor in-and-out traffic or even just use the bathroom. The police were thrilled to have a property owner invested in bettering the community. And, by helping them out, I was able to secure a police presence that was motivated to keep my tenants and my property safe.

With the serious troublemakers out of my good residents' neighboring homes, I was attracting a lot of single mothers as renters, many with close ties to criminals. These guys were the lowest of the low, and because they were dealing on the street outside my property, no one would come out from behind their locked doors.

Bonnie Laslo

At the same time, I knew these men cared about the women in my buildings. The women were family: their mothers, wives, sisters and girlfriends. So I took a chance. I walked up to each and every one of them and talked to them face-to-face.

"Do you want your mom to lose her place because of what you're doing?" I asked. "Would you please help her out by taking it someplace else?"

People said I was crazy. But you know what? It worked. All of the dealers were more than happy to stop dealing drugs on that street. In asking for their help rather than threatening them, I made them part of the solution. With cooperation from the Mayor, law enforcement and even the criminals themselves, we were able to get the street quieted down. People started coming outside. We had made the area safe enough for people to get to know each other, and for children to play in. In place of law enforcement, my residents asked the city for speed bumps to help keep their children safe. This was a nice change.

Soon my single-mother tenants started organizing babysitting trades so that they could get jobs. They worked together, made

The police were thrilled to have a property owner invested in bettering the community. And, by helping them out, I was able to secure a police presence that was motivated to keep my tenants and my property safe.

friends and even started having cookouts. All this happened in a place where, previously, no one had even dared to walk outside. My tenants started cooperating with each other. And together, they rebuilt their community.

In real estate, your properties are like your children—and your tenants are the babysitters. Your tenants will care for your property as you care for them. My tenants take it upon themselves to improve their homes, installing new flooring without being asked, painting the walls without being asked. I take care of my tenants, and they take care of their homes and stay in them longer.

We had a fire in one of my buildings, caused by arson. When I showed up with my family and team to assess and fix the damage, my tenants were already at the site working to clean it up, even though most of their apartments were not affected as badly. My tenants were not just standing by, waiting to see how I would solve the problem; they wanted to help make it easier on me to fix the problem. During the week of the fire, my tenants and team worked right alongside me until everything was done. *Without being asked.* And even though every penny they had was hard-earned and precious, my tenants bought drinks to cool us as we worked.

Cooperative business is about more than helping a community of entrepreneurs; it's about empowering consumers so that they too can become *part* of that community. Many real estate investors forget that happy, satisfied residents are perhaps the most important component in any real estate venture. Most don't recognize that their tenants are already playing on their team, simply because they choose to rent from them. How well is an investor's team going to play in the real estate market if acknowledgement and support of *all* the team's players is missing?

When residents of my properties have peaceful, well-kept, safe places to live, they become more than just tenants; they become Home Guardians. They watch over and improve their homes, and build communities around my properties. They are less likely to cause damage or problems, or forget to pay the rent – because they feel like a vital member of a community.

My tenants made me financially free. They gave me the amazing life I live today. If anyone deserves my help, it's my tenants. I educate them in any way I can, opening up the management office after hours to give free advice on everything from opening a checking account to creating a resumé. I help them repair their credit, determine if they qualify for assistance and counsel them in starting their own businesses. Whatever they are seeking, I mentor them in finding it. And I help them do something that most real estate investors would never dream of doing: I help my tenants learn how to buy their own homes.

People think I'm crazy to do this. Most have never heard of a real estate investor teaching her tenants how *not* to be tenants anymore. After all, my business is buying and holding properties for rental income. But it's the right thing to do. I believe that everyone deserves to own their own home, especially those people on my team that help me live the life of my dreams.

When you understand that you can directly affect your consumers' lives, you become financially free very quickly.

And you know what? It's great for business. For every tenant I help on the path to home ownership, there are twenty more tenants waiting to sign a lease with me. By creating a team of Home Guardians and empowering my consumers, I enjoy consistent one-hundred-percent occupancy in most of my properties – one of which I have maintained for close to thirteen years.

When you understand that you can directly affect your consumers' lives, you become financially free very quickly. When you are in cooperation with your consumers, your business is recession-proof. Many of my colleagues and friends are going broke, living off lines of credit and wondering how they will survive. Yet when the real estate market "sank," I didn't feel a ripple. They would say I am lucky, but I'm the common denominator. For years I thought my colleagues were handling their businesses in the same way I was. Turns out they were living the high life, participating in risky real estate flips and focusing only on themselves, not on their consumers. I'm a firm believer in giving more than you get. When you follow this principle, *your business can be recession-proof, too.*

If working cooperatively can transform the scariest neighborhoods into supportive, safe communities, think what it can do for your business! Your consumers are part of your team. Empower them to be the best they can be, and your *team* will be the best it can be. Which also makes YOU the best you can be. That's the lesson I've learned—and continue to live.

Bonnie Laslo is the author of two books, Hobby Millionaire *and* You Know You're a Real Estate Investor If.... *guides to real estate investing. She is also the creator of the "Hobby Millionaire Coaching Program," a boot camp for aspiring real estate investors. She built her wealth and nationwide real estate empire from the ground up beginning in Florida, where she is known as Gainesville's "Queen Bonnie." For more information about Bonnie, her books or her coaching program, please visit www.HobbyMillionaire.com.*

Conclusion

Ruby Yeh

Now that you've read heartwarming stories of love lost and found, motivating stories of childhood dreams fulfilled, inspiring stories of triumph over tragedy, adversity, disability and disease—now that you have read all of the amazing transformational stories in this book—now, it's *your* turn.

We hope that you are so moved, so inspired, and so energized after reading this collection of stories that you will take the first step on your own journey to greatness...today. It's time for you to find and pursue your own dream, so that one day soon, somebody will ask *you*—how did you do that?

Let this book be your guide, your refuge, your paperback friend. If you ever feel down, if you ever feel as though you can't, or shouldn't or won't be allowed to do that thing you've always wanted to do, come back to this book and let your favorite stories remind you that you *are* worth it and you *can* do it.

And when you get to the top of your "mountain," let us know about it. You too can be a shining example of limitless possibility. We want to hear *your* personal story of transformation. Go to www.YinspireMediaFacebook.com and let us know how you got from wishing and hoping to living and breathing your grand vision for your life—every single day.

Meet the Creators of *How Did You Do That!*

Gail Kingsbury

For the past twenty years, Gail Kingsbury has played a central role in the personal and professional development industry, planning and orchestrating seminars and events for dozens of top speakers, trainers and celebrities in small venues, stadiums and everything in between. Gail got her start in the industry with Brian Tracy and later went on to work with Tony Robbins, coordinating his Certification event in Maui and the well-known Financial Destiny event. Through her work with Robert Allen, Jay Abraham and Harry Pickens, she became a master at event and speaker marketing.

Gail went on to launch Business Events International, managing speakers and event marketing for celebrities such as Deepak Chopra, and built one of the top five conference planning websites on the Internet. After selling her company, she helped T. Harv Eker launch his first book, Secrets of the Millionaire Mind, *which hit number one on the* New York Times *Bestseller List in its first week. Gail then took on event development for his Peak Potentials Training, and worked directly with Harv to help him create some of the most amazing events in seminar industry history. Her passion for witnessing positive transformation in peoples' lives drives Gail to continually do whatever it takes to be, as Mark Victor Hansen says, "a difference maker who makes a difference." Gail lives in Central Oregon with her three daughters.*

Ruby Yeh

A former Silicon Valley entrepreneur and Fortune 500 executive, Ruby Yeh is the founder of Yinspire Media and Alive! Network, cutting-edge new media companies producing next-generation multimedia books that offer a multi-sensory reading experience including text, audio and video. She is the creator of the best-selling collaborative book, The Law of Business Attraction.

In her early Silicon Valley career, Ruby helmed multi-million-dollar international divisions of start-up software companies. She was always an innovator, even while working in major corporations, and took her extensive new market and product development experience to the role of entrepreneur, fulfilling her passion to create empowering technologies for "real people." Ruby built her first online community for Internet newbies in 1996, FolksOnline.com, and went on to innovate several award-winning Internet applications and services, including community software for interactive TV developed by an angel-funded, Silicon Valley start-up that she founded.

Ruby's mission is to help people transform their lives and fulfill their highest dreams. She does this by helping visionary messengers share their powerful stories and knowledge with the world through new media technologies.

We invite you to enjoy the
How Did You Do That! MULTI-MEDIA book.

It's an online version of this book where you can
hear and see the authors through AUDIO and VIDEO.

We offer you a GIFT section of 20+ pages from the
Multi-media book at:

www.HowDidUDoThat.com

If you wish to buy the complete Multi-media copy,
please use this coupon code to receive a substantial discount.

Coupon Code – Book2

If you like our Multi-media book format,
we also welcome you to experience another book
called *The Law of Business Attraction* at:

www.LawOfBusinessAttraction.com

If you wish to buy the complete Multi-media copy of this
book, please use this coupon code to receive a substantial
discount.

Coupon Code – Book1

We also invite you to share your experiences of our
books with our Community on our Facebook Fan Page at:

www.YinspireMediaFacebook.com